·LONDON·
AND THE
VICTORIAN
RAILWAY

·LONDON·
AND THE
VICTORIAN
RAILWAY

DAVID BRANDON

AMBERLEY

First published 2010

Amberley Publishing Plc
Cirencester Road, Chalford,
Stroud, Gloucestershire, GL6 8PE

www.amberley-books.com

ISBN 978 1 84868 228 3

British Library Cataloguing in Publication Data.
A catalogue record for this book is available from the British Library.

Typesetting and Origination by FONTHILLDESIGN.
Printed in the UK.

CONTENTS

INTRODUCTION 7

THE IMPACT OF THE RAILWAYS ON LONDON 15

CASE STUDY – EUSTON 33

CASE STUDY – PADDINGTON 41

THE EARLY DAYS OF THE UNDERGROUND RAILWAY 45

RAILWAYS & SUBURBAN GROWTH 61

RAILWAYS AND THE PURSUIT OF PLEASURE 75

THE SUPPLY OF COAL AND FOOD AND DRINK 83

RAILWAY CRIME 91

THE EARLY DAYS OF RAILWAY BOOKSTALLS 107

LINES TO THE CRYSTAL PALACE 109

SHERLOCK HOLMES AND LONDON'S RAILWAYS 113

LONDON'S VICTORIAN RAILWAYS IN ART 117

BIBLIOGRAPHY 125

INTRODUCTION

The author has been fascinated by the history of London and the history of railways for many more years than he cares to tell. He has already written a number of books on both subjects and therefore he jumped with delight when the opportunity came along to write a book about the impact of the railways on London from the 1830s to the end of the nineteenth century. Initial elation turned to a more circumspect assessment of the task ahead as its enormity and complexity became evident. Only in a much larger volume would it be possible to do full justice to the relationship between London and its railways in these years. Therefore it was decided that this book should aim to be a 'taster'; an introduction for the general reader to a selection of aspects of the subject, supported by a bibliography as a pointer for those who want more detail.

We live today in a world of hyperbole but it is no exaggeration to say that railways revolutionised the world, totally upsetting previous notions of time, distance and speed. Railways can fairly be said to have started the revolution in communications which continues even today. They created a nation out of the disparate parts that made up the British Isles. They did more than any other factor to bring about and to confirm the domination of London over British politics, culture and most other aspects of her life.

In the nineteenth century, London became the commercial and financial centre of the world and the world's leading city. It was also the capital of the British Empire which reached its apogee in the last quarter of the century. London had the most shops and the biggest shops, the worst traffic congestion and the largest number of people. During the century, the population grew by over three-and-a-half million. The spread of the urban sprawl was enormously assisted by the development of London's extensive surface and underground railway system – the two processes fed off each other. London also had some of the most noxious slums, areas of poverty, deprivation and despair. Britain was 'The Workshop of the World', her wealth burgeoning with the spread of industrialisation supported by the ideology of political economy. It took great pressure from below to exact reforms which began to tackle public health issues and working and housing conditions, for example. Contrasts between rich and poor were more concentrated and evident in London than elsewhere. London could be said to have been the epitome of the 'Two Englands' identified in literature by such writers as Thomas Carlyle and Benjamin Disraeli.

Henry Mayhew and J. Binny capture the dual character of London very effectively in the Introduction to the *The Criminal Prisons of London* published in book form in 1862: 'Viewing the Great Metropolis as an absolute world, Belgravia and Bethnal Green become the opposite poles of the London sphere – the frigid zones, as it were, of the Capital; the one icy cold from its exceeding fashion, form and ceremony; and the other wrapt in a perpetual winter of withering poverty. Of such a world, Temple Bar is the unmistakeable equator, dividing the City hemisphere from that of the West End...' This theme of counterpoint and division is taken up by Freidrich Engels in *The Condition of the Working Class in England* (1845): 'Hundreds of thousands of men and women drawn from all classes and ranks of society pack the streets of London. Are they not all human beings with the same innate characteristics and potentialities? Are they not all equally interested in the pursuit of happiness? And do they not all aim at happiness by following similar methods? Yet they rush past each other as if they had nothing in common...The more that Londoners are packed into a tiny space, the more repulsive and disgraceful becomes the brutal indifference with which they ignore their neighbours and selfishly concentrate upon their private affairs. We know well enough

'Over London' by Gustav Dore. The artist emphasises the drab uniformity of working-class housing in London and how the railway viaduct dominates the area it passes through.

that this isolation of the individual is everywhere the fundamental principle of modern society. But nowhere is this selfish egotism so blatantly evident as in the frantic bustle of the great city.'

In the last decades of the nineteenth century London was still the capital of the greatest empire in the history of the world but there were many signs that the days of its, and Britain's, pre-eminence, were numbered. The costs of running and policing were outstripping the economic benefits that the Empire was designed to provide for Britain. Several European powers as well as the USA and Japan were embarking on imperial adventures of their own. More seriously, they were also engaged in rapid industrialisation and doing so without having to undergo the bitter trial and error experience that its pioneering role in the process had enforced on Britain. The unification of Germany had created a potent economic and increasingly a naval and military competitor right on Britain's doorstep. A slap in the face, observed by the rest of the world, was her poor showing in the Boer War (1899-1902). A searing indictment of the inadequacy of existing social policy was revealed when an alarmingly large proportion of young, mostly working class men, recruited to fight in that war, were rejected on medical grounds. Labour unrest, the unresolved Irish 'problem', the increasing acrimony around the issue of women's political rights – all these were evidence of severe political and social stresses. Going although not yet totally gone was the supreme optimism and confidence in Britain's role in the world manifested by so many of her 'movers and shakers' earlier in the century.

London is an organism which, like all living matter, is in a process of continuing and continuous change. Now even the meaning of the word 'London' changed. At one time 'London' had been synonymous just with the City but the term now referred to the City, to Westminster, the West End and all the other built-up areas insidiously spreading their tentacles into Surrey, Kent, Middlesex, Hertfordshire and Essex, and into each other. London supported large numbers of wealthy people who, for a century or more, had been increasingly moving from its filth, clamour and underlying menace to villages on and beyond its periphery. Uxbridge, Harrow, Chiswick, Dulwich, Enfield and Epping come to mind. There were many others and they were increasingly drawn into London's rapacious maw.

As will be seen, the railways both responded to this process and assisted it. However, the railways were by no means the major reason for London's growth. For the suburbs to develop and for railways to be built to connect them to the centre, there had to be jobs in central London for workers to go to as well as other attractions to draw them in. The jobs had to be sufficiently well-paid to enable the workers to afford the train fares. They also needed to be able to pay the rent for the houses in the suburbs which in turn speculative builders had to be convinced represented a worthwhile risk for their expenditure. No part of this tangle of processes would have been possible without an enormous increase in the overall wealth of London. Explaining why that economic growth occurred presents an issue beyond the present remit. Suffice it to say that the key to understanding London's headlong outward expansion in the Victorian era lies with that economic growth, certainly not with the creation of the railways *per se*.

This book attempts to identify ways in which the railways had an impact and influence on London. Railways and Victorian London seem inseparable but it is easy to forget that in the nineteenth century, the majority of the haulage of people and goods around

'Towards St Paul's'. A classic view towards St Paul's Cathedral but Dore has portrayed the extraordinary traffic gridlock which was a feature of parts of London before the railways were built.

London's streets was still performed by horses and most people got around on foot. The first underground railway opened in 1863, others followed as did surface railways but as far as public transport was concerned, the horse bus and horse tram were pre-eminent right into the 1890s. It is not denying the dramatic influence of railways on London to argue that their role in providing transport around the metropolis itself in the nineteenth century was only one and not necessarily the most important of their effects. Another effect, easy to ignore, was that the coal and general merchandise which arrived in London by rail had to be delivered from goods depots to the consumers and this of course was almost all done using horses. Until the internal combustion engine became a practicality, the number of horses and people engaged in various ways of working with them, increased steadily. In the 1870s, Gustav Dore produced an impression of traffic congestion in a view looking down Ludgate Hill towards St Paul's. There are dozens of horses in this picture of traffic gridlock. The confusion is not helped by the fact that someone is trying to drive a herd of sheep through the city's streets.

Some of the railway companies at first displayed little interest in what we might describe as 'short-haul commuters'. The London & Birmingham Railway when it opened had its first station up the line as far out as Harrow, the Great Western its first at Ealing. Other companies, such as the Great Eastern Railway, were only too happy to be agents of demographic change and substantially to assist the development of suburbs with more of a lower middle-class and skilled working-class character such as Stratford, Leyton and Leytonstone. Just how quickly some of these places developed is shown by the growth of West Ham. Between the censuses of 1801 and 1901 its population rose from 6,500 to 267,400. It cannot be said that this growth and similar growth elsewhere was caused by the railway but unquestionably it was greatly facilitated by it. Historical causation is always complex.

Railways were the product of the received wisdoms of the Victorian era – economic individualism and *laissez-faire*. The bafflingly complex network of lines which came to serve London was never a system in any real sense. It was not planned. Instead it was the haphazard outcome of a desire of some investors to get rich quick and of others to find a safe and steady lodging place for their savings. It was also the product of virtually unbridled competition. Insofar as Parliament intervened in the 'public interest', whatever that means, it was with reluctance and a light touch. The financing of railways and the trade in railway shares contributed to London's leading national and increasingly international role in banking, insurance and commerce. The number of jobs in the City increased exponentially at the same time as its population emptied out. Imposing and prestigious office blocks sprung up, sometimes replacing ancient churches that had stood on the same sites and symbolising the triumph of Mammon. Old coaching inns redolent of the golden age of the stage coach, closed down, were converted for other use or were demolished. They had no place in the age of the train.

The promoters of London's first railway of significance, the London & Greenwich, designed it to compete with steamboats on the Thames and with stage coaches, largely for the regular commuter traffic between the two places. The line was not a huge success. It won little commuter traffic initially but found, to its surprise, that it could tap into the leisure business. Many Londoners found it cheaper to take a steamboat one way and a railway train the other for an afternoon out in Greenwich. London's railways were on their way. So much was to follow. As the *Building News* said in 1862, 'The invasion of

The London & Greenwich Railway ran on a viaduct of the sort which became such a feature of the approaches to stations like London Bridge, Victoria and Waterloo.

the Metropolis by the 'Steam Horse' has, during the last quarter of a century, produced changes, not only in the physical features of the metropolis, but also in the manners, customs, mode of living, and even in the thoughts of its inhabitants, which are almost incredible. For a century previous to the year 1834, stagnation was the order of the day; but then came the locomotive into London, and all was changed.'

Even more extravagant was the claim made by *Building News* in 1870: 'What would London do now without a railway? What would become of the immense holiday crowds who are regularly whirled over the country, fifty miles and back, in a single day with eight hours at the seaside, if the railways were suddenly to shut up shop? Brighton and Southend became seaside extensions of the metropolis, while Birmingham and Bradford could appropriately be described as outposts of the City. Physical contiguity or even proximity ceased to be necessary prerequisites to the kinds of activities, whether involving business or pleasure, associated with cities. The network of interdependency linking the farthest corners of England with the metropolis that Defoe had celebrated with his 'Tour' reached its logical culmination with the creation of the Victorian railway and telegraph systems. It could be said that all England was a suburb of London, and each part of that real Greater London proceeded to specialise not only in its material but its aesthetic, intellectual, and emotional production; knowing that whatever it did not provide could be had a short railway away.'

Right: The engineer Richard Trevithick demonstrated his steam locomotive called 'Catch-me-who-can' on a circular railway close to the site of the future Euston Station in 1808. Unfortunately while plenty of people turned up and paid good money to view this novelty, the locomotive was too heavy for the track and was eventually derailed.

Below: This extraordinary 4-horsepower locomotive 'Impulsoria' was demonstrated at Nine Elms on the London & South Western Railway in 1850. This machine was invented by Clemente Masserand who claimed that it could provide a very cheap form of locomotion on branch lincs.

THE IMPACT OF RAILWAYS ON LONDON

The First Railways Come To London

The first railway to give a real hint of the revolutionary economic and social potential of this new-fangled form of transport was the Liverpool & Manchester Railway, opened in 1830. This line between the two premier cities of north-west England was designed from the start for steam haulage except for a short length at the Liverpool end where it dropped down sharply to the level of the River Mersey. It was the first major railway of significant length and it quickly proved a boon to Liverpool's business community who, among other benefits, could now obtain coal much more cheaply. Manchester men relished the drop in the price of raw cotton imported initially through Liverpool and which was now being transported by the railway. These possibilities had been a consideration when the line was being promoted. What was totally unforeseen was the substantial passenger traffic that quickly developed between the two cities. This, as might be expected, included people travelling on business but what quickly became obvious was that there was also a demand from those who simply wanted to use this radically fast and apparently safe form of travel for what would now be called 'leisure pursuits'. It was only about thirty-five miles between the two cities and now, for the first time, it was so much quicker and cheaper that it became realistic to travel from one to the other, not only perhaps to visit friends and relatives but just for the stimulus that comes from travelling around and visiting new places. In 1838 over 600,000 passengers journeyed by train between the two towns. The success of the Liverpool and Manchester made the world sit up and take notice.

The Liverpool & Manchester was by no means Britain's first railway. Plateways, waggonways and primitive railways were to be found in many locations, their function primarily being the movement of coal and other heavy minerals from pithead or quarry to the nearest navigable water. The evolutionary development of steam engines used for such purposes as driving machinery or pumping water out of pits into locomotives that could haul themselves and attached loads around on rails was very much a case of trial and error. One of the most successful of the early steam locomotive engineers was George Stephenson and his locomotives made an impact on the Stockton & Darlington Railway opened in 1825. Day-to-day haulage in the early years was, however, largely performed by horses. These developments largely passed London by. Its earliest line was the Surrey Iron Railway opened in 1803, a simple waggonway which linked the industries located around Croydon and the Wandle Valley with the River Thames at Wandsworth.

England's road system, extensively upgraded by the nineteenth century, had London as its hub. This fact, combined with the navigability of the Thames and easy access to the sea plus a lack of valuable minerals in the area, meant that railway developments around London lagged behind those taking place particularly in the areas which were the centre of an industrial revolution based on coal and iron. It was therefore at the comparatively late date of December 1836 that London's first railway was opened. This was the London & Greenwich, just four miles long and promoted largely as a line for commuters. Its terminus was near the southern end of London Bridge, handy for City workers. This line established a practice widely associated with many of London's subsequent railways. This was the compulsory purchase and demolition of large numbers of existing buildings as the lines made their way towards the London termini. The London & Greenwich was built entirely on viaducts. The structures used for the approach depended largely on the terrain. Viaducts were a feature particularly of the area to the south of the Thames. Cuttings and tunnels were characteristic of the lines threading the Northern Heights on their way into King's Cross, St Pancras, Marylebone and Euston stations. Liverpool Street managed to combine cuttings and viaducts. The land acquired by the London & Greenwich was relatively cheap and much of the line ran across largely unused land. As railway development continued through the century, the price of land rose and it became a very pertinent consideration in the minds of those promoting schemes. It is worth noting that in 1831 the densely-populated part of

London & Greenwich Railway.

the London region occupied about 18 square miles and was home to a population of around 1.65 million.

A Grand Central Station for London?

Even a person unfamiliar with the Metropolis could look at a map and conclude that none of its major stations are located in central London, with the possible exception of Charing Cross and, being generous, Victoria. The rest are very much peripheral. While this which may have meant lower land values for the sites involved, it made them inconvenient in all sorts of ways for the companies concerned and for their customers. The idea of one or two large central stations acting both as termini and exchange points for the various main lines serving London was mooted early on. It kept popping up right through to the 1880s as London's road traffic congestion grew ever worse. The Royal Commission of Metropolitan Termini recommended in 1846 that big stations be kept out of central London, defined as an area known as the 'Quadrilateral'. This was largely because of the even greater congestion that it was envisaged would be generated around any such central stations. Other factors included the cost and other problems

The proposed terminus of the 'London Grand Junction Railway' at Skinner Street, Clerkenwell. This was just one of many schemes for tackling road congestion in London but it would have been at the expense of carving a swathe through areas of densely-packed industrial, commercial and residential property.

associated with acquiring the land necessary for such an undertaking and in an age of largely untrammelled business competition, the difficulty of managing and reconciling the possibly conflicting interests of half-a-dozen or more railway companies.

In 1846, Charles Pearson, a busy City solicitor and MP who we shall meet again on matters concerning the Metropolitan Railway, produced plans for a station to serve five companies. At that time extensive slum clearance was taking place along the Fleet Valley which meant that an area stretching from Clerkenwell Green to Ludgate Circus was being opened up for redevelopment. On 11 May, Pearson gave a speech to an august audience at the Guildhall in the City about his project and he even provided a model for them to mull over. His plan took account of the ongoing discussions about the building of a road bridge across the valley of the River Fleet. This was to become a reality in 1869 when Holborn Viaduct was opened.

Pearson's passenger station was designed to serve lines entering London from the north and it was bisected by Victoria Street which later became part of Farringdon Street. The northern approaches were along what later became the Metropolitan Widened Lines from King's Cross. Pearson's scheme for the central station included the building of the necessary roads and a comprehensive redevelopment of the entire area. Unfortunately for Pearson, the Royal Commission's report of 1846 came out soon afterwards and this combined with a general lack of interest from the Corporation of London rendered the project dead and consigned it to historical obscurity. As originally planned, a garden suburb several miles out of London would have been built for those working people displaced by the building of the station. The line itself would have been enclosed in an arcade with a street for vehicular traffic running along the top.

Pearson's idea was replaced by looking at ways of improving communications between the various stations scattered around the periphery. It was around the issues of growing road congestion and the need to link the stations more effectively that the idea of underground railways in London had their genesis. The so-called 'Inner Circle' sub-surface line, completed in 1884, served the purpose of linking most of the main line termini with the important exceptions of Waterloo and London Bridge, south of the Thames, and Fenchurch Street and Holborn Viaduct Stations which perhaps did not really qualify as serving main lines.

The barring of main line railways from central London became a principle. Even so, there was a proposal by the London & North Western Railway in 1863 for a terminus at Leicester Square which would have replaced Euston while the South Eastern Railway toyed with the idea of a terminus of its own in the same location ten years later. There was near-gridlock in central London along many of the most important streets and at their intersections for much of the period from the 1840s to 1900. The dispersal of the railway termini at least prevented what would have been even more appalling road congestion around one or more central stations.

EARLY LINES THAT MIGHT HAVE BEEN

It is a somewhat glib generalisation to say that the Victorians thought big. Some Victorians certainly had vision. Most people simply had to get on with grinding out a living with little time to spare for greater things. The railways had gestated before

Victoria ascended the throne but they really came to fruition during her reign. The London & Greenwich Railway opened in 1836 and was well-received. The British economy was about to enter a speculative bubble called 'The Railway Mania'. Here we look at a number of schemes for railways in the capital that never came to much beyond being pipe-dreams. For all that, they indicate much about the mind-set of the engineers and architects of the Victorian period.

Following swiftly in the wake of the London & Greenwich was a scheme for the line to be extended to Gravesend. No sooner was this suggested than the idea became dead in the water as large numbers of choleric but highly influential retired admirals made their objections clear. The line would have crossed Greenwich Park near the Royal Naval College and the Queen's House, a piece of desecration which could never be allowed to happen, no matter how decorative the promoters promised they would make the line as it passed through the Park. It was 1878 before a railway crossed Greenwich Park. It did so by tunnelling under it. Another associated line was to be the Westminster, Deptford and Greenwich Railway. This was to leave the London & Greenwich in the Deptford area and pass through Peckham, Camberwell and Kennington before terminating at an impressive station on the south bank of the Thames near Westminster Bridge. At the London end, the line would have run on arches beneath which were elegant shops while further out small dwellings would be housed underneath the arches. This rather grandiose scheme failed to gain parliamentary approval.

When the London & Birmingham Railway opened its Euston Station, it was inconveniently placed at the extreme north of the built-up area of Central London. In 1835, some time before it opened, a scheme was afoot for a 'London Grand Junction Railway' running from Camden Town where it would leave the L & B through St Pancras, Clerkenwell and Holborn to the north bank of the Thames at Blackfriars. A modified scheme had the railway running along a viaduct although only as far at its southern end as Newgate. Nothing directly came of this project.

James Clephan was a visionary architect who wanted to build a railway, ten miles long, linking all the main line termini. This scheme was nothing if not ambitious because it envisaged trains running on some sort of silent pneumatic principle along elevated terraces on either side of brand new roads with homes above and shops below. This line which would cross the Thames and have a link with the London Docks would have obviated the need for a central terminus. So grandiloquent in its vision, the name for this project was actually rather under-stated. It was to be the 'London Railway'. It never became anything other than a twinkle in the eyes of Clephan.

The ponderously-named 'London Connecting Railway and Railway Transit Line' envisaged a line joining all the major stations and connecting with a central terminus in the not very central location of Elephant & Castle. The most novel feature of this proposal was an arrangement whereby the various sections of the line would meet by the Thames where goods trains and ships could exchange cargoes. This project never proceeded beyond a proposal.

The 'Central Terminus Company' proposed the building of three, not one, enormous central stations dominating the north bank of the Thames. In the 1850s a plan emerged for the building of a 'Metropolitan Super Way'. This was to be an elevated line joining all of central London's most important districts and running in an iron tube supported by columns. Helpfully, each of its stations was to contain a sub-post-office.

There is no doubting the enormous impact created by Joseph Paxton's 'Crystal Palace' in Hyde Park as it glittered and coruscated when the sun came out after a shower of rain. The world was thinking 'crystal' and it is not surprising to learn that a 'Crystal Way' was proposed to connect the City with Oxford Circus and Seven Dials with Piccadilly. An atmospheric railway was to run just below ground level with a glass-enclosed shopping arcade above and trains that would somehow allow passengers to alight without the vehicles actually stopping. No one could understand the principle on which this worked and it was soon consigned to the out-tray of history. Sir Joseph Paxton himself designed what he called 'The Great Victorian Way', a structure of glass containing railway lines, a road and shops and houses. It would have been ten miles long and its route would have been very similar to that later taken by the Inner Circle Line. Perhaps the most outrageous of all the schemes for railways in Central London was that which proudly boasted that it avoided all the trouble involved with compulsory purchase and demolition. 'The Thames Viaduct Railway' was to run a line next to a viaduct built along the middle of the River Thames.

These various schemes, all more-or-less crazy, have to be seen in the context that to influential Victorians, almost anything seemed achievable by harnessing science and technology along with determination. This belief, combined with the fact that some railway lines provided very favourable returns for their investors probably accounts for the lurid imagination and cavalier disregard for what was actually possible that underpinned these various concepts.

DISRUPTION CAUSED BY RAILWAY CONSTRUCTION

The construction of London's railways was hugely disruptive where they affected those parts of the metropolis which were already built up. Bodies, public or private, with responsibilities for the provision of utilities raised objections for the way the construction of many railways disturbed what was already a complicated spaghetti-like system of subterranean pipes, sewers, gas-mains, etc. Roads and bridges had to be demolished or reconstructed. All manner of disputes and legal wrangles arose around these issues as indeed they did when domestic and other built property needed to be bought and, as usually happened, demolished. Another emotive issue occurred when human remains in churchyards and other burial places needed to be moved.

The Metropolitan Board of Works was established in 1855 as a body with local government responsibilities across the whole of London. The parliamentary act under which it was introduced gave it very extensive powers and as a newcomer, it was determined to flex its muscles. It engaged in a battle royal with the District Railway concerning the building of the Victoria Embankment which included the railway as well as a vital part of London's new sewage system. In the 1870s the Board proved powerful enough to force the Midland Railway Company to foreshorten its new Somers Town Goods Depot next to St Pancras Station to allow for a widening of Euston Road.

The legal, financial and other considerations involved in railway building in densely developed parts of the metropolis meant that where lines were planned to run just below the ground, as far as possible they followed the paths of existing roads or utilised open spaces. It was agreed that an ideal solution would be to combine the construction of

Excavations for the building of the Metropolitan Railway give us some idea of the disruption caused by railway construction in built up areas of London.

railways with the building of the new roads that were desperately needed to ease road congestion and 'open up' some of London's most notorious criminal rookeries. The building of the Victoria Embankment has already been mentioned. With this and its extension to Mansion House as Queen Victoria Street in the early 1870s, the Board and the District Railway came to agreement on an economic use of resources and managed an improvement to the road and rail system. Another proposal for a new street being touted urgently was one to run from Tottenham Court Road to Charing Cross. While it was agreed that this should follow the same pattern, it never happened, at least in the form initially envisaged.

Of the major London termini, the approaches to Paddington were among the easiest from the financial, legal and engineering points of view. Not for nothing was the Great Western's line out of Paddington described as 'Brunel's Billiard Table' but it was also helpful that most of the land involved was owned by the Bishop of London. The approach and purchase of land for Victoria demonstrated how much easier it was when the three railway companies concerned, the London, Brighton and South Coast, the London, Chatham and Dover and the Great Western had to deal with very few landowners, the Marquess of Westminster dominating this area. Men of such wealth and influence had the clout to squeeze very favourable terms for themselves out of the railway companies. This made such projects expensive but at the same time relatively quick and easy to negotiate. By contrast, the negotiations to acquire the approaches to the site of Broad Street and Liverpool Street stations were very convoluted because of

Building the extension from London Bridge to Charing Cross on viaducts meant the demolition of large amounts of property although not, fortunately, St Saviour's Church, later Southwark Cathedral seen in the background.

the large number of landowners involved. The attitude of landowners varied. Few were as adamant that the railways would not enter their domain as the Duke of Bedford. He wanted to keep his Bloomsbury Estate exclusive. They say that every man has his price but the Duke could not be bought.

Where it was consonant with engineering and other factors, the railway companies tried to buy cheap land and this often involved the demolition of the properties along the proposed route or on the sites which were designated for stations, sidings and other kinds of railway use. Cheap land was often occupied by cheap housing, usually rented by people without money and therefore with little influence. Much of this property consisted of dire slums, the seats of crime, disease and despair. So the railways incidentally became a factor in the process of slum clearance. The problem, however, was that there was not necessarily any legal requirement for the railway company to re-house the displaced residents. They were simply decanted into the neighbouring districts where the housing was little, if any better, and which then just became even more overcrowded, noxious and miserable. As *The Times* stated, 'The poor are displaced but they are not removed. They are shovelled out of one side of the parish, only to render more overcrowded the stifling apartments in another part'. From 1874 the legal conditions attached to the purchase of land obliged a railway company to make some provision for those who were displaced. An example where this happened occurred in the late 1890s when what became the Great Central Railway required land for its Marylebone Station and associated sidings. They had to erect six blocks of tenement flats, misleadingly called Wharncliffe Gardens, to house 2,690 of those people who had occupied housing on the site. It was stated that 6,200 people were displaced. Many of those unable to secure a place in the tenements simply spilt over into the already notoriously overcrowded slums of the Lisson Grove district.

On some occasions the railway companies were required to make cheap workmen's fares available to and from inner-city suburbs to which, in theory at least, some of the displaced residents had moved. It was not unknown for companies to ignore or evade any legal requirements concerning the people who were displaced. Overall the railways probably caused more harm than good so far as the dwellings of the poor were concerned. We are talking substantial numbers because it is estimated that railway-building in London in the second half of the nineteenth century caused the demolition of houses containing at least 120,000 residents. It has to be said that there were plenty of hard-nosed people (probably railway shareholders) who argued that it was unfair that the cost of making provision for those displaced by demolition should be shouldered by the companies themselves who would have had little option but to defray that cost in the price of its tickets.

A Metropolitan Line steam-hauled train as depicted by Dore. Location is probably Baker Street.

The Railway Viaducts of London

In many places, the viaducts along which the railways approached their London termini became dominant features of the urban landscape. Sometimes they also had a devastating effect on the local community by cutting a swathe through an established district not only involving demolition of dwellings and other buildings but worsening environmental pollution and causing huge disruption for those still living and working close by. A viaduct and even a cutting could create a physical frontier where none had existed before. This might have the effect of breaking up the cohesion of a community. Trains leaving the eastern end of London Bridge Station travelled for some distance over low brick viaducts which had been extended outwards as additional lines were laid. To this day the underneath of these viaducts constitutes a dark, dingy and dangerous no-man's land dividing parts of Southwark and Bermondsey from each other. The existence of these viaducts cast a pall on an already blighted area from which it has never fully recovered.

The railway, so much a factor in facilitating the growth of the British economy in the nineteenth century and in bringing people the empowering effect of (relatively) cheap travel, especially for pleasure, also had consequences which emphasised the socially divisive nature of capitalism. Some of these viaducts leading into London provided a grandstand view of just what the largely unregulated economic development of the time was doing to the environment especially for those less skilled and lower-paid members of the workforce whose labour power contributed so much to making the overall increase in wealth possible.

Charles Dickens with his customary awareness of social reality, especially at the lower end of the social order, provides an immortal description of the approach to London over railway viaducts in 'Dombey and Son' (1869): *Everything around is blackened. There are dark pools of water, muddy lanes, and miserable habitations far below. There are jagged walls and filthy houses close at hand, and through the battered roofs and broken windows, wretched rooms are seen, where want and fever hide themselves in many wretched shapes, while smoke and crowded gables, and distorted chimneys, and deformity of mind and body, choke the murky distance. As Mr Dombey looks out of his carriage window, it is never in his thoughts that the monster who brought him here has let the light of day in on these things: not made or caused them...it was so ruinous and dreary.*

Decayed slum areas seem to have held a fascination for Dickens who held forth in some detail about Agar Town and Somers Town. These districts were bisected by the lines of the LNWR and the Great Northern as they made their way towards Euston and Kings Cross respectively. The area was a mishmash of poor quality housing and small industrial premises. Once again in *Dombey and Son* he paints a vivid picture: 'Every garden has its nuisance but every nuisance was of a distinct and peculiar character. In one a dung-heap, in the next a cinder-heap, in the third, which belonged to the cottage of a costermonger, was a pile of whelk and periwinkle shells, some rotten cabbages and a donkey: and the garden of another...had become a pond of thick green water.' He went on to describe the mountain of refuse which acted as the centrepiece for this foetid district which also contained assorted industries each of which stamped its character on the area. These included the sheds of rag collectors, knackers' yards, small factories manufacturing soap and boiling bones for glue and also brick kilns and a gas works.

This festering slum had been wedged between the lines of the LNWR and the GNR and the size, shape and nature of the area was such that no developer was tempted to pull it down and start all over again. It was simply in some kind of slowly declining time-warp. It had never been much in the first place. However it was ideally suited for the purposes of the Midland Railway who built St Pancras station and the adjacent Somers Town goods depot on it in 1862.

It had been quickly realised that the building of a railway could create a barrier or frontier which might change the nature of the area through which it passed, frequently for the worse. The London & South Western Railway proposed a line on a viaduct from Waterloo to the Thames at Bankside. This line would have crossed Waterloo Road, Blackfriars Road and Southwark Bridge Road and it was recognised at the time that it would constitute a brick barrier cutting off much of Southwark, Lambeth and Kennington from the Thames and Central London. The line was not built. Nearby, the LSWR's wide viaduct into Waterloo completed in 1848 was generally agreed to have closed off streets, eroding the integrity of the area and causing a run-down of the district especially of the buildings close to the viaduct, the arches of which attracted lowlife like flies round a jam pot. Railways did not themselves create slums but they strongly influenced the character of the inner-city districts through which they passed.

Messrs Mayhew and Binny, referred to previously, in *The Criminal Prisons of London* provide a marvellous impression of the approach to London over this self-same set of viaducts: 'What an odd notion the stranger must acquire of the Metropolis, as he enters it by the South-Western Railway! How curious is the flash of the passing

Dore gives a stark view of one of the purposes to which the arches under the viaducts was put.

Vauxhall Gardens, dreary with their big black trees, and the huge theatrical-looking summer house, built for the orchestra and half-tumbling to decay; and the momentary glimpse of the Tartarus-like gas-works, with their tall minaret chimneys, and the red mouth of some open retort there glowing like the crater of a burning volcano; and the sudden whisking by the Lambeth potteries, with their show of sample chimney-pots, and earthen pans, and tubing, ranged along the walls; and the minute afterwards, the glance at the black rack-like sheds, spotted all over with the snowy ends of lumps of whiting, thrust at intervals through the apertures; and then the sickening stench of the bone-boilers, leaking in through every crevice of the carriage; and the dreary-looking attics of houses as the roofs fly past...'

RAILWAYS AND THE INDUSTRIES OF LONDON

London is not usually thought of as the hub of Britain's Industrial Revolution. However, its sheer size and the cumulative wealth of its citizens created demand as did its myriad functions and diversity and its importance as a major seaport. Even so it comes as a surprise to learn that in 1861 15% of the jobs in manufacturing industry in England and Wales were to be found in London. Traditionally most of the industrial concerns were small-scale. They came in an infinite variety of trades and were producing mostly, sometimes entirely, for the London market. Raw materials came in by road, sea or canal before the arrival of the railways. The railways never gained a monopoly of supplying London's raw materials needs.

In the nineteenth century some very large industrial enterprises opened in London, depending from the start on the support of the railways. The Gas Light & Coke Company had a huge plant at Beckton on the north bank of the Thames. This opened in 1872 and was connected to the Great Eastern Railway as well as having an extensive internal railway system with around seventy miles of track. The Royal Arsenal at Woolwich was a huge concern which had boasted a horse-worked internal tramway as early as 1825 but gained a narrow-gauge steam-powered system in the late 1860s. A standard gauge link was made to the South Eastern Railway's North Kent line and the Arsenal's internal railway system eventually sported a third rail so that standard-gauge main line rolling stock could operate over it.

The construction of locomotives and other rolling stock is a heavy industry of a type not commonly associated with London but five major railway companies had factories engaged in this activity. The first was that of the London & South Western Railway at Nine Elms, opened in 1839; the Eastern Counties (later Great Eastern) Railway at Stratford in 1847/8; the North London Railway at Bow (1853); London, Tilbury & Southend Railway at Plaistow and the London, Chatham & Dover Railway at Longhedge, Battersea in 1862.

By far the most impressive of these installations was Stratford Works where the Great Eastern Railway eventually built nearly all its locomotives and other rolling stock. It was the centre of a strange, isolated railway settlement, originally called Hudson Town after George Hudson, one-time chairman of the Eastern Counties Railway. It had houses and other facilities for a community of railway workers and their families many of whom migrated there after leaving agricultural work in East Anglia and Lincolnshire.

Like a number of other large companies, the Great Eastern tried to produce as many as possible of the consumable items it needed in-house and for that reason the works included impressive facilities for producing such things as timetables and handbills. Bow Works was not far from Stratford but it established an impressive reputation for its output. The Nine Elms works outgrew its site and its carriage and wagon business was transferred to Eastleigh near Southampton in 1891 followed by locomotive building and repair in 1910. This was a particularly significant event because the closure of Nine Elms was symptomatic of the decline of Battersea's earlier sizeable industrial quarter. It was the last heavy engineering factory so close to central London. Longhedge Works was never very impressive. Located not far from Nine Elms, it closed entirely in 1911, its work being transferred to Ashford in Kent.

A small number of private locomotive manufacturers were to be found in London. Early on the scene was the company of Messrs Braithwaite & Ericcson who entered their locomotive 'Novelty' in the Rainhill Trails on the Liverpool & Manchester Railway in 1829. It failed to complete all the tests but still made an impression, not least because it was the first steam locomotive to be reliably timed running a mile in less than a minute. They built a number of locomotives for export to the USA but ceased operations in 1841. The largest of the other companies was George England's Hatcham Ironworks in New Cross. Between 1840 and 1872 they assembled about 250 locomotives but when they closed that was the end of private locomotive building in London. There were many private firms engaged in supplying the railway industry with such things as signalling equipment. Saxby & Farmer of Kilburn were a nationally-known company. Other London firms supplied items as diverse as lifts, carriage fittings, water closets and printed handbills.

Although London did have large factories, it was not primarily a centre of heavy industry. Its characteristic industrial workplace was small; on a workshop rather than a factory scale. There is little evidence in the nineteenth century that proximity to a railway was a major consideration in the location of new, large factories in London. Having no coal or iron ore of its own, London depended on water or rail for bringing in these raw materials and there was much short-haul movement of rail-born coal in particular around the capital, delivering to places near the industrial consumer. Railway and other operators of street cartage brought in raw materials and carried away the finished products of a thousand and one small manufacturers. Breweries required coal in substantial quantities but few, if any, had their own rail connections. Industries such as flour-milling do not seem to have considered railways as being particularly important factors in the location of their premises. In the case of gas works, railway provision was often a serious consideration, Beckton already mentioned, being a good example. Electricity generating plants were generally located where coal could be brought in by water. The railways of Britain were excellent movers of heavy, non-perishable cargoes such as coal, iron ore and stone. Vast quantities of coal from South and West Yorkshire and the East Midlands arrived in London by rail but London's industries with their generally small consignments for outward dispatch were of the kind where the railway played a marginal rather than a central role. By contrast, the margins of London's canals and navigable rivers were frequently characterised by industrial development. Generalities about the interaction between railways and manufacturing industries that might be made about provincial cities do not necessarily apply to London. Its very special role in Britain's affairs meant that it came to be dominated by service industries.

EMPLOYMENT

The absence of large railway works, except those at Stratford, meant that London never really had its Wolvertons, Crewes, Gortons or Springburns. These were towns or suburbs in the provinces which were dominated physically, economically, socially and politically by the presence of one or more large factories engaged in providing the locomotives, rolling stock as well as the million and one other items needed to keep railways operating. In such places, much of the housing and the infrastructure of the settlement were frequently provided by the railway companies who, with private suppliers, were by far the major employers.

There were districts in London which were enclaves of concentrated railway activity. Five come quickly to mind: the Camden, Kentish Town, Kings Cross and St Pancras area; Old Oak and Willesden Junction; Battersea and Clapham Junction; Bricklayers Arms and New Cross; Stratford and Bow. All of these with the exception of St Pancras had engine sheds and these installations were always highly labour intensive. Several of them had railway works and others had goods depots, shunting yards and/or carriage sidings. Additionally, London obviously had huge numbers of railway stations, large and small, with many having substantial and often very large workforces. The number of signal boxes was quite baffling by modern standards and, collectively, they provided many jobs. There were hoards of track maintenance workers as well as others in clerical, administrative, supervisory and managerial roles. Many railway workers were engaged in catering and hospitality activities. Additionally there were other working people who indirectly gained their employment from the railways. Cab-drivers and those who worked in bookstalls are examples. Many carters and omnibus drivers and guards greatly depended on business generated by the railways. For much of the time between the 1830s and 1900, substantial numbers of men were employed in railway construction work. Meaningful statistics on railway employment in this period are hard to come by. For all that, the railways were only one among an extraordinarily vast and diverse range of sources of employment in these years and clearly constituted a significant part of the London labour market.

Railway work was not particularly well-paid and management practices were usually far from paternalistic. Some companies used an almost military style of discipline. Hours were long and they often involved shift work round the clock. However, a worker who kept a good disciplinary record could expect a job for life and, if he or she was ambitious, the possibility of promotion was very real. Engine drivers consciously saw themselves, and were seen, as members of the labour aristocracy. Signalmen were usually people of very steady temperament who often had the justified reputation of being self-taught men of learning. A stationmaster, even of a small station, was a man of some standing in the community. At places like Paddington, Victoria or Kings Cross, the stationmaster was a senior manager with the dignity and prestige thought to be appropriate to such a position. Such officials would often parade in top hat and tails to see off the main trains of the day. It was likely that such a man had started on the bottom rung of the ladder of railway employment. One enormous perk enjoyed by directly-employed railway workers was free or cheap travel on the company's lines to and from work. This enabled many of them to live in locations quite distant from their actual places of employment, an advantage open to them unlike dock workers, for

Allright! The guard gives the rightaway.

Another railway accident. A cartoon having the caption, 'Just as the station master had given the signal for the train to start, a frightful collision took place'. Cartoonists and other humorists found a rich source of inspiration in just about every activity associated with the railways.

example, and many of them took advantage of it. Gradually privilege tickets became available on the lines of other companies, not just for work purposes but also for leisure and other uses.

Censuses make it clear that large numbers of railway workers were not indigenous to London. Some moved from the provinces to the London area on promotion or in the hope of advancement. Those existing railway workers who migrated to London almost always continued to work for the same company such was their loyalty even if it was sometimes a grudging one. The Great Western Railway had many employees in London, especially on the operating side, who were from Wales, the West Midlands and the West Country and it must have been amusing to hear their accents contrasting with those of their London colleagues. The Great Northern had substantial numbers of workers who originated from the West Riding of Yorkshire and the Great Eastern enjoyed the services of many who hailed from Norfolk and Suffolk. Such rustics often earned the amused and even affectionate contempt of their London peers who always thought of themselves as being far more streetwise and sophisticated.

The railways were a factor in the increase of social mobility and the complex division of labour which were features of the developing nineteenth century economy. Railways brought people together physically and by means of the printed word. In that sense they were demotic. However it could be argued that overall they were also socially divisive. Not only were passenger trains themselves and the public facilities on railway stations strictly graded along the lines of cost and therefore of class but the railways, especially in London, encouraged the development of housing areas outside Central London demarcated along the lines of income and status. In the building of London's railway system, the claims of the disenfranchised whose lives were disrupted or even destroyed were rarely allowed to obstruct what they were told was the necessary onward march of progress. The railways were generators of economic activity. London was a much richer city at the end of Victoria's reign than it had been in the 1830s and it cannot be questioned that the railways were a significant contributor to that enrichment. Unfortunately, the increased wealth was not necessarily shared out with the most deserving or hard-working obtaining their fair share.

CASE STUDY — EUSTON

The first major inter-city company to arrive in the capital was the London & Birmingham Railway which built its Euston station at the bottom of a gradient of about 1 in 70, so steep that for the first seven years trains had to be hauled up to Camden attached to a continuous cable powered by stationary steam engines. Later locomotives were more powerful but the banking of many trains out of Euston was a feature of the station's working until the end of steam operations. Banking involved a locomotive buffering up to the rear of a train and using brute force to assist the locomotive at the front and shove it and its train up Camden Bank. The station opened on 20 July 1837. It got its name because it occupied land once owned by the Fitzroy family whose country seat was Euston Hall in Suffolk. It could be argued that Euston was the London end of the first trunk railway in the world.

Euston was not the original choice of the company as the location for its terminus. Islington, Tyburn, Maiden Lane near King's Cross and Camden Town had all previously been given serious consideration. Just to the west of the station, land was set aside for what was originally intended to be the Great Western Railway's London terminus. The idea of a joint station in this early stage of the railway age was an attractive one, offering the possibility of economies for both companies. Negotiations on this move fell through. This is probably just as well as the companies later found themselves directly competing for passengers travelling to Birmingham, Wolverhampton, Chester and Merseyside. They would never have been contented bedfellows.

The original station was a simple one with an 'arrivals' and a 'departures' platform under an overall roof or train shed. Far more imposing was Hardwick's symbolic Doric propylaeum or portico and its associated lodges which declared to anyone passing on the Euston Road that here was a place where trains left for distant places and, of course, arrived from the same. This grandiloquent statement in stone cost £35,000 and was a piece of brash triumphalism totally superfluous to the company's business of running trains and making a profit for its shareholders. The latter were outraged when they heard how much it had cost. Later development hid the Doric Arch from the Euston Road, thereby largely robbing it of its purpose and only adding fuel to the resentment of those who thought it should never have been built in the first place. Sir John Betjeman described the Euston Arch as 'a gateway from England's capital and heart, London, to her stomach and toyshop, Birmingham'.

The famous Doric arch which greeted the traveller arriving at Euston.

A two-storey building contained such amenities as toilets and waiting rooms. First class passengers had their own private facilities, those reserved for second class passengers were distinctly second best but a lot better than the provision for third-class passengers which was non-existent! Some of the wealthiest first-class passengers would arrive at the station in their private carriages which were then loaded on to flat wagons and attached to the scheduled train while their horses were placed in horse boxes. These passengers could remain in their carriages during the journey if they so wished. In the arrogant manner of the idle rich, they often arrived only minutes before the train was due to leave and then complained when the train left late having been delayed by the last-minute necessity to attach their carriages to the wagons and make arrangements for the horses.

The London and Birmingham at the time of the opening of Euston only boasted three arrivals and departures each day and these served Harrow, Watford and Boxmoor. On 17 September 1838 the line was completed to Birmingham with a service of nine trains in each direction taking nearly six hours to complete the journey. A year later, two railway hotels were opened at Euston. One, the 'Victoria' was a fairly humble establishment while the 'Euston' catered for first-class passengers. It had 141 bedrooms and only closed in 1963 when the whole of the station was rebuilt for the imminent inauguration of electric services. Although GWR trains never graced Euston, the Midland Counties (later Midland Railway) obtained running powers over London & Birmingham metals from Rugby for its trains from the East and North Midlands and Yorkshire. These started operating in 1840. Right up to the last days of the old Euston, Platform 9 was still known as the 'York', an example of unwitting historical evidence.

As traffic developed, the station expanded its platforms, buildings and services, occupying some of the land reserved for what would have been the Great Western's part of the station. Euston developed like Topsy – it just grew. It became a somewhat haphazard and complicated jumble of buildings of different ages and, over the years, the station proved to be increasingly inconvenient and inefficient for the purposes of handling growing numbers of passengers and the trains in which they travelled. This was ironic because what became the central core of the station was the magnificent Great Hall opened in 1849. This was a combined concourse and waiting room and provided a grandiose focus for the station which increasingly belied the rather ramshackle nature of much of the rest of the complex. The architectural features of the Great Hall have often been described and no attempt will be made to do so here with one exception. This refers to the ceiling of the Great Hall which was decorated with plaster bas-reliefs. These bas-reliefs apparently symbolised places served by the trains of the London & North Western Railway, now the station's owner. They were in pairs and were an impressive size, being 10 ft long. The author remembers picking them out as a child. He had no knowledge of or interest in what they symbolised. What did catch his juvenile interest was the fact that the female figures were both bare-breasted and very full-breasted. He returned to the Great Hall time and time again and often had reluctantly to tear himself away from the female sculptures to fulfil his ostensible purpose at Euston which was train-spotting. For the record, the bas-reliefs represented London, Liverpool, Manchester, Birmingham, Carlisle, Chester, Lancaster and Northampton.

It was all go at the old Euston. A few examples will suffice. On 29 May 1856, Herbert Spencer (1820-1903), the philosopher, was mugged by footpads and had his watch stolen in the station environs. In 1860 the band of the St Pancras Volunteers was given permission to use the crypt below the station when they wanted to practice as long as they didn't frighten the passengers. In 1864 the Queen's Waiting Room which was superbly furnished and fitted suffered the indignity of being converted into a parcels office. Soon afterwards the refreshment counter in the Great Hall was closed on Sundays because it had 'become a public resort for loungers and others' during the hours in which the pubs were closed.

The London & North Western Railway was not pleased when the Midland Railway Company opened up its own independent route to London and arrived with such an overbearing presence just along the Euston Road at St Pancras. St Pancras opened in 1868 and its arrival stung the LNWR into making various improvements at Euston which was now looking distinctly old and tired by comparison. The ground in front of the station was opened up and two small entrance lodges erected which are there to this day. On the quoins of these lodges are incised gilded letters giving the names of principle destinations that could be reached by the company's trains. Even at this time, some of these places were far more conveniently served by the trains of other, competing, companies.

Disparaging comments about Euston led to a further enlargement in 1892 which gave the station 15 platforms and effected improvements especially to train working. Despite these developments the opprobrious comments about Euston continued and the board of directors was poised to embark on a much more thoroughgoing reconstruction of the station for which legal powers were obtained in 1900. The economic problems associated with the Boer War intervened and the plans were put on hold. Reconstruction of Euston was postponed until the 1960s. This reconstruction was nothing if not comprehensive but the rebuilt Euston that emerged, while it may have been more

Exterior of the engine house at Camden, London & Birmingham Railway.

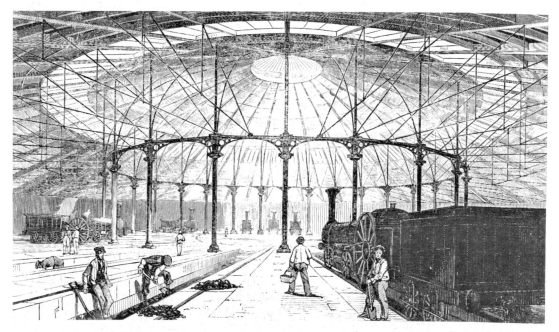

Interior of the engine house at Camden.

efficient, quickly became one of Britain's most disliked large railway stations, aping in many ways although not quite achieving the amazing utilitarian repulsiveness of its near-contemporary, the rebuilt Birmingham New Street.

Euston came to be dominated by long-distance services to the West Midlands, to North Wales, Merseyside, Lancashire, the Lake District and Scotland and never had the intensive short-haul suburban provision that featured at so many other major London termini. Train-spotters will remember Euston for having a sense of bustle but actually not that many trains although in steam days those that did turn up often had large and impressive named locomotives hauling them. The LNWR was not at first especially interested in serving the inner suburbs that were developing in the second half of the century but stations at Chalk Farm and Kilburn High Road opened in 1851, at Willesden Junction in 1866 and at South Hampstead and Queens Park in 1879. The nearest thing in the nineteenth century to a suburban network out of Euston was a service to Watford which developed in intensity as the areas around the stations *en route* were opened up for residential and other developments.

The coming of the railways opened up the realistic possibility that people could travel round the country for pleasure visiting places and buildings of historical, architectural and other interest. While such expeditions were not cheap, they attracted sufficient numbers of people of middling income to create a demand for guide books and other items containing material of a topographical nature. One such publication was *Rides on Railways* by Samuel Sidney. This takes the reader on a rail-borne perambulation

King's Cross Station soon after it opened in 1852 replacing a temporary station nearby.

Looking up the ornate staircase of the Midland Grand Hotel which acted as the façade of the Midland Railway's St Pancras Station.

over the lines of the London & North Western Railway out of Euston. It is chattily informative and probably less valuable to the historian of railways than to scholars of the culture of the 1850s when it was published.

Sidney makes some interesting comments on Euston. 'It is only to be regretted that it was not possible to bring the station within a few yards of the New Road, so as to render the stream of omnibuses between Paddington and the City available, without compelling the passenger to perspire under his carpet-bag, railway-wrapper, umbrella, and hat box, all the way from the platform to the edge of Euston Square.' He describes the arch as 'very imposing and rather out of place' but continues: '...Euston, to be viewed to advantage, should be visited by the grey light of a summer or spring morning, about a quarter to six o'clock...At the hour mentioned, the Railway passenger-yard is vacant, silent, and as spotlessly clean as a Dutchman's kitchen; nothing to be seen but a tall soldier-like policeman in green, on watch under the wooden shed, and a few sparrows industriously yet vainly trying to get breakfast from between the closely-packed paving-stones. How different from the fat debauched-looking sparrows who throve upon the dirt and waste of the old coach yards! Presently, hurrying on foot, a few passengers arrive: a servant-maid carrying a big box, with the assistance of a little girl; a neat punctual-looking man, probably a bankers clerk on furlough; and a couple of young fellows in shaggy coats, smoking, who seem by their red eyes and dirty hands, to have made sure of being up early by not going to bed. A rattle announces the first omnibus, with a pile of luggage outside and five inside passengers, two commercial travellers, two who may be curates or schoolmasters, and a brown man with a large sea-chest.' He continues for several more pages, very much in the same vein. In so doing, he brings Euston of the 1850s to life.

CASE STUDY — PADDINGTON

The London & Bristol Railway, progenitor of the Great Western Railway, required a London terminus and a site in the Paddington district was by no means the only option available. Consideration was given to sites at Pimlico near Vauxhall Bridge and Victoria and legal powers were obtained for the GWR to make a junction with the London & Birmingham Railway in the Wormwood Scrubs area and share its station at Euston Square. This proposal must have rankled with their engineer, Isambard Kingdom Brunel, whose grandiloquent vision certainly would not have included asking another railway company if they would be kind enough to provide them with access to their station. In the event, negotiations with the London & Birmingham broke down and parliamentary powers were obtained for a line to a terminus at what is now Bishop's Bridge Road, slightly to the west of the future Paddington Station. It was on the site of what was later to be the GWR's massive Paddington Goods Depot. The GWR's first London station opened on 4 June 1838, trains running only as far as Maidenhead. Through services to Bristol over Brunel's brilliantly engineered route started on 30 June 1841. This station then expanded as traffic developed but it was an unimpressive terminus for a route that contained prodigies of the science and art of civil engineering such as Wharncliffe Viaduct, Maidenhead Bridge and Box Tunnel. For all that, the complex of buildings contained a shed in which locomotives were serviced. It was designed by Daniel Gooch and was probably the first to be designed as a roundhouse. The locality of this first Paddington Station was still semi-rural and the parish authorities concerned were somewhat confused and overwhelmed by the sudden explosion of traffic and human business and activity on their patch once the station was open. One of the activities which aroused concern was that of male travellers urinating over the bridge into the nearby Regent's Canal. Some did so quite ostentatiously, arousing the ire or possibly the envy of members of the parish council. At that stage the GWR provided no toilets at the station.

Every dog has its day, so the saying goes, and this rather mean structure had its day when Queen Victoria arrived at the station on 13 June 1842, having been staying at Windsor Castle and taking the train to London from Slough, the nearest railhead. Daniel Gooch, the GWR's Locomotive Superintendent had himself driven the locomotive of the Royal Train. Perhaps he felt the need to show off and he managed to achieve an average speed of no less than 44 mph. This was a greater velocity than had ever previously been achieved by the young Queen which was not surprising because it was actually her

The first station at Paddington.

Interior of the second Paddington station fortunately, with enlargement and modifications, still with us today.

first journey by train. She arrived in London sufficiently flustered by the experience for Albert discreetly to request that any future journeys on the GWR should be undertaken less speedily (and by implication less hazardously).

In February 1853 the directors of the GWR decided to build a permanent and grander terminus. Brunel handled most major aspects of the design of the station but collaborated with the eminent Matthew Digby Wyatt, member of an esteemed dynasty of architects, particularly on the roof and its supporting columns. Wyatt was also responsible for the delightful oriel windows in the trainshed. The roof with its extensive use of iron and glass drew on the example of the Crystal Palace, designed by Joseph Paxton, which had recently housed the Great Exhibition in Hyde Park. Brunel had sat on the Committee which, from a number of entrants, chose what they thought was the building most suitable for housing the Exhibition. At first the Committee was unable to decide among the submissions and so it had put forward a design of its own. The Committee came up with what looked like an unnecessarily long, wide and low railway station. For once, Brunel had lost the plot because his contribution was an enormous dome so dominant that it seemed to be pinning the rest of the building to the ground. There was something of the Gothic cathedral in the new Paddington. It had a nave with aisles and even transepts, all under a towering roof of iron and glass and the effect was light and airy. Although not quite complete, the station opened to the public on 16 January 1854. Enlarged with the addition of extra platforms, today's Paddington would still be instantly recognisable to Brunel and Wyatt.

A few months after the station opened, the Great Western Royal Hotel, designed by Philip Hardwick, began operating. This hotel acted as the station's frontage onto Conduit Street (later Praed Street) but had not been part of Brunel's grand scheme for Paddington Station. It was a large and architecturally eclectic building, the first of the major railway hotels built in conjunction with London's large railway termini. By general agreement, it provided the best facilities among London's hotels at that time and it was, for a while, the largest hotel in Britain. The GWR had its eyes on what it was hoped would be the lucrative and prestigious traffic in well-to-do passengers travelling to the far west of England, to Ireland via ports in the west of Wales and, if Brunel had had his way, also embarking in those ports on steamships designed by himself and heading across the Atlantic to the USA and thereby competing for trade with Liverpool. Only the best hotel accommodation should be provided for such people. By contrast, large numbers of rather insalubrious small hotels opened up in the shadow of Paddington, a feature of the streets adjacent to many of London's large terminal stations.

When originally opened, Paddington was almost on the edge of the continuously built-up mass of the Metropolis. The GWR needed to minimise the inconvenience caused by the relative isolation of Paddington and therefore it was a major player in the negotiations leading to the opening of the Metropolitan Railway. The first section of this line ran from nearby Bishop's Road to Farringdon on the western fringe of the City. Services started in January 1863. The GWR's participation meant that the line had to be built with mixed gauge track as the Great Western's trains were then all of Brunel's broad gauge rolling stock. Broad gauge trains ceased operating in March 1869. In 1865 trains began running on the Hammersmith & City line. This left the GWR main line at Westbourne Park. GWR services from several outer-London places began to run onto the Metropolitan which completed a line through the nearby Praed Street station to Gloucester Road in 1868.

When the line into Paddington opened, it passed through districts which were still rural. Acton and Ealing, for example, were mere villages. The GWR showed little interest in serving such places and the first station out of London was West Drayton, over thirteen miles out. As mentioned elsewhere (railways and suburban growth), the opening of a station at Ealing led to rapid building development in the vicinity. Even despite continuing suburban growth, the GWR in the nineteenth century gave the impression of being far more interested in long-haul passenger traffic and it was served by more long-distance trains than any of the other London termini.

The broad gauge (2.14m) was a typically grandiloquent gesture on the part of Brunel. He argued vehemently for its superiority in terms of speed, safety and carrying capacity and disparaged everyone else's standard gauge lines as 'coal-cart railways'. The sight of a broad gauge express travelling at speed must have been something to stir the soul of all but the most prosaically-minded. There are those who have always argued that actually Brunel got it right and it was the others that were mistaken. A broad gauge network would, for example, certainly be able to handle large modern containers more effectively. However the fact is that with the rest of Britain's major railways going for the standard gauge (1.44m), it became increasingly anomalous for the GWR to bury its head in the sand and think that they would eventually come round to its way of thinking. So it was that the first trains running over mixed gauge tracks arrived in Paddington in the second half of 1861. Brunel was long in his grave in Kensal Green Cemetery before the GWR directors took the decision to abandon the broad gauge completely. Even then, with so much investment in broad gauge rolling stock and infrastructure, it was not until 21 May 1892 that the last broad gauge express train left Paddington for Penzance. This departed Paddington at 10.15 am and was appropriately headed by the locomotive proudly named *Great Western*. This was a superb 4-2-2 designed by William Dean and which had only entered service in 1888.

Some of the atmosphere of Paddington was neatly captured by Sir John Betjeman (1906-84) in his description of Paddington in *London's Historic Railway Stations*: 'The undergraduates of Oxford used Paddington; and so did Public Schools at Eton, Radley, Marlborough, Shrewsbury, Malvern...hunting people got out at Badminton; carpet manufacturers at Kidderminster; coal owners at Cardiff; jewellers at Birmingham; valetudinarians at Torquay, Leamington, Cheltenham, Tenbury Wells and Tenby; sailors at Plymouth, Devonport and Falmouth; organists used it for the Three Choirs Festival at Worcester, Hereford and Gloucester. The Welsh who seemed so often to be in trains, use it all the time.' Although Betjeman was obviously writing in the twentieth century, what he said could equally well apply to Paddington in Victorian times. The station did always have an indefinable air that its trains served the cathedral cities of the West, the mellow limestone settlements of the Cotswolds, the dreamy spires of Oxford, the gorgeous red cliffs of Teignmouth and Dawlish, the balmy littoral of the Cornish 'Riviera' and mysterious far-flung places in West Wales beyond Swansea and Llanelli. It was always served by more long-distance trains than the other London termini. For many, it was always the most romantic of London's big stations.

THE EARLY DAYS OF THE UNDERGROUND RAILWAYS

The Metropolitan Railway

London can claim many firsts. One of the most notable of them is the world's first underground railway. This was the Metropolitan Railway running at first over a route nearly four miles long from Bishops Road at Paddington to Farringdon Street on the western edge of the City. It opened to great acclaim on 10 January 1863 and was soon carrying over 25,000 people daily. Sober assessment over the next few months suggested that it was going to be a solid success, at least in terms of passengers carried and street traffic congestion eased. The Metropolitan Railway proved that underground railways could be a viable financial operation but could also generate the travel habit, meaning that people would now make journeys because transport was available who previously would have stayed at home.

However, it had been some time in coming and had excited much opposition and controversy. Two people should be given the credit for their vision, persuasiveness and tenacity because without them it would not have happened when it did. They were Charles Pearson, a City lawyer and human dynamo who espoused many worthy causes and got things done, and John Hargrave Stevens, an architect and surveyor. Pearson died shortly before the line opened. He had vehemently argued that cheap railway travel was a way of enabling London's poorer citizens to live away from the insanitary, soot-laden and generally noxious conditions which made up most of Central London.

Among the developing factors which influenced the arguments for the building of some high-speed transport link between the developing suburbs along the New Road (now the Marylebone and Euston Roads) and the City was the establishment from the late 1830s of important railway termini at Paddington, Euston and Kings Cross and the determination of the Midland Railway to open one on the same axis at St Pancras. These stations urgently needed better communication with other parts of the Metropolis, not least with the City. Buses plied between Paddington and the City but became caught up in road congestion. London in the 1850s was booming but in danger of sclerosis. It was a victim of its own success. Increased prosperity, more residents, more visitors, more business – the road system was reaching saturation and beyond. Urgent action was needed. It was clear that main line railways were not going to be allowed in Central London and some radical solution to road traffic gridlock was urgently required. No link between the various major termini could possibly be built at surface level or on viaducts through Central London.

Various schemes for underground railways had been put forward from the 1830s only to come to nothing but in 1854 parliamentary approval was given for a 'Metropolitan Railway: Paddington and the Great Western Railway, the General Post Office, the London & North Western Railway, and the Great Northern Railway'. Stevens was appointed architect and John Fowler the engineer. However the railway speculation 'bubble' had burst, the costs of the Crimean War had to be defrayed and little finance was immediately available meaning that there was a delay before construction work began.

The line was built on the then novel 'cut-and-cover' idea whereby a deep trench or subway was excavated along which the tracks were laid and which was then partially roofed over. Roads or buildings could then be erected over the path of the line. To minimise the expense involved in the compulsory purchase of buildings along the route or of tunnelling under other buildings which might be damaged and where compensation might have to be paid, as far as possible the line ran under existing roads. Those affected were particularly Praed Street and New Road now divided up as Marylebone Road and Euston Road. In many places the tracks were open to the sky to allow the smoke to disperse. Obviously while the construction work was going it caused great disruption to road traffic. It also involved the diversion of the spaghetti of pipes for the various utilities that run unseen below the surface of the Metropolis. The covered way resulting from these efforts was built wide enough to house the broad gauge track required by trains of the Great Western Railway. It had been agreed that their trains and those of the Great Northern Railway would have access to the metals of the Metropolitan so mixed gauge track had to be provided. At Farringdon Street what was then the terminus was built on the site of the City Cattle Market which had earlier been moved to Copenhagen

Early GWR broad gauge underground train at Paddington.

Fields, north of Kings Cross. A spur ran into the basement of the new London Central Meat Market which was completed in 1868. The Metropolitan and the GWR, the two companies involved, clearly had their eyes on the business opportunities offered by this venture.

Considering the scale of the civil engineering works and their pioneering nature, the building of the Metropolitan went off remarkably easily. The only major incident occurred in June 1862 when the Fleet River, the valley of which was followed by the railway between Kings Cross and Farringdon, burst through retaining walls and flooded the workings. On the southern section of the line from Kings Cross to Farringdon there were fewer existing roads to follow easily. Official figures stated that just 307 people were displaced as the result of the demolition of their dwellings. Other contemporary estimates put the figure as high as 12,000.

From the start there had been concerns about the smuts and smoke that would be produced by the steam locomotives pulling the trains. People living close to the line complained that their garden shrubs would be killed by sulphurous fumes created by the trains. Stations like Baker Street which were entirely subterranean contained a poisonous and almost impenetrable fug which caused travellers to cough, splutter, expectorate and complain impotently. The sooty miasma proved a helpful environment for pickpockets. The carriages were lighted by oil lamps which emitted a foul smell and dripped on passengers. The light flickered capriciously. Those regular travellers who wanted to read often stuck candles on to the inside of the carriage near where they were sitting. Early underground travel was not for the faint-hearted.

It was in anticipation of the problems caused by operating steam locomotives below ground that an attempt was made to produce a locomotive that was 'smokeless'. The idea was that a white-hot firebrick would heat the water in the locomotive's boiler and produce the steam needed for propulsion but without any smoke while the locomotive was operating along the underground parts of the line. Robert Stephenson (1803-59) designed and built an experimental locomotive in 1861. He was without doubt a great and resourceful engineer but the resulting locomotive was not one of his greater successes. True, the machine produced very little smoke but it also produced very little steam and it was all it could do to pull itself around, let alone haul a train. It was an impressive-looking machine but its looks belied its performance and it quickly disappeared from public view, not, however, before having gained the derisive nickname 'Fowler's Ghost' because no one was sure whether or not it actually existed. In the event, Daniel Gooch, the locomotive superintendent of the GWR designed a class of powerful 2-4-0Ts for use on the Metropolitan. They had open cabs and life can have been no sinecure for the drivers and firemen. Relations between the GWR and the Metropolitan became fraught and the latter company introduced its own 4-4-0 tank engines built by Beyer-Peacock which proved to be highly successful. They had apparatus which allowed them to condense much of their steam. At least that's how the theory went.

In spite of apocalyptic predictions that the building of underground railways would disturb the Devil, who would then wreak his revenge in the ways that only he knew how, and equally dire warnings to the effect that tunnels and cuttings would collapse, crushing those brazen and stupid enough to travel on it, the line from Paddington to Farringdon was an almost total success. *The Times* newspaper had added its weight to the Jeremiahs with sinister allusions to 'passages inhabited by rats, soaked with sewer drippings' and the possibility of being poisoned by gas given off by ruptured mains. The line was a success except in the case of one Sarah Dobner, a 56-year-old woman who had a bronchial condition greatly exacerbated, it was believed, by what the coroner's court described in 1867 as 'the suffocating atmosphere of the Underground Railway'. There certainly was an acrid fug for much of the time on the stations and the issue of adequate ventilation continued to excite controversy and was only finally ended with the electrification of the sub-surface lines. The Metropolitan actually claimed that the sulphurous conditions were beneficial to those with asthmatic and bronchial conditions. Fug apart, the Metropolitan Railway proved to be a safe and quick form of transport. Interestingly, when the line opened, the company refused to allow smoking on its trains but pressure built up over the years and smoking coaches were introduced in 1874.

The success of the Metropolitan Railway concentrated minds and was followed by the opening of the Hammersmith & City line in June 1864. This was built by a nominally independent company with the support of the GWR and the Metropolitan and was designed to feed into the existing line of the latter company. The track was mixed gauge and it connected Hammersmith with the Metropolitan at Paddington, thereby giving districts in West London direct access to the fringe of the City. One of the quirks of London's railway history resulted from the building of this line was that it spawned a branch which linked up with the West London and the West London Extension Railways. With a connecting link to Victoria, this meant that trains of the London, Brighton & South Coast Railway appeared in Paddington and Great Western broad gauge trains in turn graced Victoria, a piquant thought for today's railway enthusiasts.

The Hammersmith & City ran through some largely rural districts and where stations were opened in these areas, examples being Latimer Road and Goldhawk Road, it established the practice associated with underground railways whereby speculative builders moved in soon afterwards and housing and other development quickly followed. Where the line had stations in existing built-up areas, it tended to have the effect of changing their social character. Ladbroke Grove was an example. The large and elegant terraces of this district were already degenerating into multi-occupancy. The opening of the line accelerated this process as well as leading to much infilling with smaller housing which came to be occupied by people from the lower-middle classes. The population of Hammersmith burgeoned as the result of the arrival of the Hammersmith & City and later the District Line. Housing development followed on the opening of the District Line from Hammersmith.

The Metropolitan had become busier in 1 October 1863 when Great Northern Railway trains began running to Farringdon Street. At the same time, broad gauge trains of the GWR commenced operating from Windsor to Farringdon. An extension had been authorised eastwards to Moorgate Street in the City. To ease traffic flows it was decided that the line between Kings Cross and Moorgate should be quadrupled and the result was the 'Widened Lines' as this stretch of line came to be known. Trains began running to Moorgate in 1865. Great Northern Railway trains ran to places in Hertfordshire as far away as Hatfield and Hitchin.

An important development was a line running from just south of Farringdon Street through Snow Hill and Ludgate Hill. This line was operated by the London, Chatham and Dover Railway Company and it opened to traffic in May 1869. It provided an important cross-London route which came to be used not just by the passenger trains of

The building of the LCDR's viaduct across Ludgate Hill provoked much controversy because it detracted from the classic view of the west front of St Paul's.

The LCDR Company arms as still visible from Blackfriars Bridge.

various companies but also by many freight trains. It was never part of the underground system although it traversed the Widened Lines north of Farringdon. It eventually became part of the Thameslink system. The LCDR's line generated much controversy in its early years because it crossed Ludgate Hill on a bridge which spoiled the much-loved view up to St Paul's Cathedral. Yet more traffic began to flow on the Widened Lines from July 1868 when trains of the Midland Railway started running into Moorgate. In 1869 the GWR ceased to run broad gauge trains on the Metropolitan Railway.

The Metropolitan Railway was the first in London to offer cheap tickets for workmen travelling early in the morning. These tickets proved immensely popular. This was in 1864. From the start the company was happy to accommodate third class passengers and indeed over two-thirds of the accommodation on its early trains was for such passengers.

Much has been made in recent years about the regenerative effect that an improved transport infrastructure can have on a stagnant or declining area. The Jubilee Line extension was an example. Proximity to the Metropolitan back in the 1860s became a major selling point in the advertisements of businesses close to its route, many of whom found that the railway brought them new customers. The Metropolitan soon became exceptionally busy. In 1865 over 350 trains left Farringdon between 5.15 am and midnight. It became beneficial to live or work near the Metropolitan.

THE DISTRICT AND INNER CIRCLE LINES

The Metropolitan Railway acted as a model for any number of schemes for further lines of the same kind. The most urgent was a line to link the various main line termini and hopefully reduce the road traffic they generated. An Act had been passed to create an embankment on the north side of the Thames with the intention of relieving the traffic gridlock along the Strand and to house a major sewer. This was the work of the great engineer Sir Joseph Bazalgette. It would economise on resources if the suggested line ran along this proposed embankment. It was intended that the line would extend the Metropolitan via the City, the Embankment, Westminster, Victoria and Kensington to Paddington. It was designed to be an inner circle railway link but it was, of course, not circular. This proposed line received parliamentary approval in July 1864. Once again, Sir Henry Fowler was the engineer. The section from Kensington to Tower Hill was called the Metropolitan District Railway. It had close links with the Metropolitan and it was intended that in due course the two concerns would amalgamate.

The line passed through some very affluent areas especially in the Kensington and Notting Hill districts and met with considerable opposition from powerful landowners. They were able to screw excessive compensation from the company. The use of cut-and-cover was more difficult in this part of London because the line cut across the grid of streets rather than going with their flow. At Leinster Gardens, Bayswater, the line was in a particularly shallow cutting and the demolition of nos. 23 and 24 could not be avoided. However the company was required to maintain the appearance of the street and so wooden screens replicating the facades of the two adjacent houses were erected and have become well-known as one of London's many oddities. The author knew someone who lived in Leinster Gardens for several years and had never realised that nos. 23 and 24 were dummy façades. They obviously did the job they were intended to do. Another curiosity which resulted from the building of the line can still be seen at Sloane Square Station. This is an iron conduit which crosses the station and contains the Westbourne, one of London's many hidden rivers.

The Metropolitan District, which we will now call the District Line, and the Metropolitan, fell out over a number of issues and the amalgamation never did take place. Worse than that, the acrimonious relationships between the two verged on the childish. The most problematical location was, predictably, the Embankment and delays, partly because the District had run out of money, meant that this section was not completed to Mansion House until 1871. The Metropolitan ran into serious problems with the cost of acquiring land in the City so much so that doubts were being expressed as to whether the Inner Circle would ever be completed. In 1879 legislation authorised the two warring companies to work together and complete the circle as well as to build a link from Aldgate to connect with the East London Railway at Whitechapel. In 1884 the latter line was completed. From the start the companies bickered over their individual share of the receipts. No love was lost when the Metropolitan started running trains from Hammersmith via Kings Cross over the East London Railway to New Cross to connect up with the South Eastern Railway and by way of a retort the District ran trains from Hammersmith via Temple and the East London Railway to New Cross Gate to link up with the London, Brighton & South Coast Railway.

The Metropolitan and the District Lines didn't just dislike each other, it was absolute mutual loathing. Their antipathy to each other descended to the level of farce. While final arrangements were being made for the opening of the Inner Circle, they entered into a dispute over access to a particular siding at South Kensington The District staked its territorial claim by running a locomotive and a short train into the siding and chaining it to the track against the possibility of assault and takeover by the Metropolitan. This was a reasonable precaution because it wasn't long before the Metropolitan came along with three of their locomotives, intent on removing the District Line's presence on the siding. A tug-of-war then ensued with the Metropolitan literally trying to heave their hated rivals off the short piece of disputed track. The Metropolitan was unsuccessful.

Early extensions of the District Line took in Hammersmith in June 1877, Ealing 1879, Putney Bridge in 1880 and Wimbledon in 1889. The District and the London, Tilbury & Southend Railway jointly owned a line connecting the District's Whitechapel terminus to the LTSR at Bow and this opened in 1902. The District line benefited from passing through South Kensington, sometimes described as 'Albertopolis', which became a focus of museums built partly with the profits from the Great Exhibition of 1851. It even built a pedestrian subway from South Kensington to Exhibition Road where the museums were housed and it developed significant leisure traffic. Another draw, access to which the District facilitated, was Earls Court with its exhibition halls and the Big Wheel, opened in 1895. This proved to be a huge draw for its entire working life of twelve years. The Metropolitan, for its part, came under the management of the bullish, even ruthless, Sir Edward Watkin. He had big ideas for it, wanting to develop it into a main line company and under his auspices it thrust north-westwards from Baker Street into Buckinghamshire. It opened to Harrow-on-the-Hill in 1880, Pinner in 1885, Chesham 1889, Rickmansworth in 1887 and Aylesbury 1892. The transport infrastructure for the 'Metroland' of the future was being built.

The East London Railway

By the late eighteenth century, there was a crying need for some kind of better way of crossing of the Thames to the east of London Bridge, particularly between Rotherhithe and Wapping. There were docks and warehouses on both sides of the river and an effective means of linking them was required. The location was not thought suitable for a bridge and so the idea gradually developed of a tunnel at this point. The problem was that no one had ever tunnelled such a distance under water and there were many people who simply thought it could not be done. The Thames Archway Company was set up with the intention of making a practical investigation. A pilot tunnel was not far off completion in 1808 when the river broke in and ruined what had already been done. The project was abandoned.

In 1818 Marc Brunel patented an ingenious tunnelling shield based on his knowledge of how the misnamed shipworm (actually a mollusc) or teredo bored through wood and confident that a machine had now been found to do the trick, the Thames Tunnel Company was established to build a tunnel, again from Rotherhithe to Wapping. Work started in March 1825. The tunnelling shield was the pioneer of all such devices and its principles are still employed in the immensely sophisticated tunnel drilling machines used today. For a period the later famous Isambard Kingdom Brunel, son of Marc, was the engineer in charge. The project proved immensely difficult and far more expensive and it was abandoned for a while but eventually opened amid great celebration on 25 March 1843. It was designed for vehicular traffic with two carriageways but it never saw use for that purpose because there was no money available for the ramps that should have been installed at either end to provide access for wheeled vehicles. At first it attracted sightseers in large numbers but the gimmick wore out and it became merely a rather grand underwater footpath decorated with many market stalls and where, it is said, ladies of the night plied their trade.

The carriageways were large and it therefore made sense for the tunnel to be used to house a railway running under the river. The East London Railway then acquired the tunnel with a view to allowing railway companies to run their trains through it on payment of a charge. In 1869 the line opened from Wapping to New Cross (later New Cross Gate) where it connected with the London, Brighton & South Coast Railway. The initial service through the tunnel was operated by the LBSCR and ran from New Cross to Wapping. In 1876 the line was extended at the northern end enabling LBSCR trains to run into the Great Eastern Railway's Liverpool Street terminus. In 1876 a short-lived through service between Liverpool Street and Brighton started. In 1880 the South Eastern Railway joined the fun with a service from Addiscombe Road to Liverpool Street through its own New Cross station. In 1884 these trains were diverted via the newly-built Whitechapel Curve to St Mary's on the joint line of the Metropolitan & District lines. A considerable amount of freight traffic passed over the East London Railway. The Thames Tunnel has had a chequered history, for many years being part of the London Underground system, but at the time of writing (2009) it is closed for engineering work which will enable it to start a new phase of its life as a crucial link improving main line rail connections between districts north and south of the river. Christian Wolmar in *The Subterranean Railway* (2004) aptly describes it as being 'built primarily because the tunnel was already there, rather than to fulfil any immediate railway purpose'. Its best days may be ahead of it.

THE STEAM-HAULED UNDERGROUND EXPERIENCE

Also in Wolmar's excellent book is a quote from the diary of the writer R. D. Blumenthal. The year is 1887 and he took a journey from Baker Street to Moorgate. It is unclear as to whether this was his first trip on an underground train but it was certainly an experience which made an impression on him. He described it as his 'first experience of Hades'. He went on: ... 'The compartment in which I sat was filled with passengers who were smoking pipes, as is the British habit, and as the smoke and sulphur from the engine filled the tunnel, all the windows have to be closed. The atmosphere was a mixture of sulphur, coal dust and foul fumes from the oil lamp above: so that by the time we reached Moorgate Street I was near dead of asphyxiation and heat. I should think these Underground railways must soon be discontinued, for they are a menace to health.'

Electrification of the sub-surface lines that have been mentioned was going to have to wait until the decade from 1900.

THE TOWER SUBWAY

The lines mentioned so far were sub-surface employing cut-and-cover construction wherever possible. The Tower Subway was a pioneer of a different sort. It was the world's first tube railway, if only for a short time. It proved that tunnels could be constructed at a level deep enough to avoid the increasingly complicated network of sewers and pipes to be found under the Metropolis. The clays underlying London were relatively easy to bore through with the technology available at that time.

Peter William Barlow was an engineer of many parts who wanted to see whether it was possible to build railways running underground in iron tubes. In 1864 his associate James Henry Greathead patented a circular adaptation of Marc Brunel's tunnelling shield. In 1868 the Tower Subway Company was formed to build a tube tunnel under the Thames from Tower Hill to Southwark. It was to be 1340 feet long and the Greathead device was to be used in its construction. The internal diameter of the tubes was less than 6ft 8 in. At its deepest, the tunnel was 66 feet below high water level. Lifts were provided from the surface. A strange windowless and claustrophobic car with maximum seating for twelve ran along a track with a 2ft 6 in gauge. Small stationary steam engines provided cable haulage and the official opening was on 2 August 1870. It was a remarkable piece of engineering but the passenger car was too small to carry a viable payload of passengers. In this form it could not be made to pay and it was decided to cut losses and convert the venture into a foot tunnel from 24 December 1870. Pedestrians paid one halfpenny to use it and in its new guise it was successful until Tower Bridge opened nearby in 1894. Passengers could walk across it for free. The two little brick-built entrances to the tunnel can still be seen and the tunnel is still *in situ* carrying water pipes. The northern entrance is at Tower Hill, the southern at Vine Street.

THE CITY & SOUTH LONDON RAILWAY

The Greathead tunnelling shield proved to be a great success and it was soon to be employed on a project of national, indeed international importance. This was the City & South London Railway which was the first major underground railway to operate in deep-level tube tunnels.

The City of London & Southwark Subway Company was incorporated in July 1884. Greathead was appointed engineer. The northern terminus in the City was to be at King William Street near the Monument and having passed under the Thames, the line would then proceed under Borough High Street and Newington Causeway to terminate at Elephant & Castle. Work began in February 1886 and in 1887 legislative approval was given to the line being extended to Stockwell, giving it a length of just over three miles. At first the intention was that the line should be cable-powered but the idea of electric traction had some appeal and so the decision was made to electrify it right from the start. Formal opening of the line took place on 4 November 1890 by which time the owners had changed their name to the City & South London Railway. Public services started on 18 December. Small electric locomotives hauled passenger cars with seats for thirty-two. It is interesting that the early cars were not provided with windows on the basis that there was nothing for passengers to see. They were noisy and claustrophobic. Not surprisingly, these cars soon became known as 'padded cells'. *Punch* magazine has always enjoyed satirising new economic and social phenomena and it referred to the line as the 'sardine box railway'. A flat fare of two pence was levied, passengers inserting their money in a turnstile. Although staff called out the names of stations, it is obvious that passengers preferred to have windows even if there was nothing to see and so later carriages were equipped with them. All stations were provided with lifts from the start, necessary for a deep-level line. The line reduced the travel time between Stockwell and King William Street by more than half.

The City & South London was a considerable although not perhaps a total success. It was extended to Moorgate in February 1900, the section from Borough to King William Street being abandoned. It says much for the difficulties encountered by the promoters that the new line had a station near King William Street at Bank. It was an awkward site and the booking hall was fashioned partly out of the crypt of St Mary Woolnoth church. This is a fifteenth century church rebuilt by Wren after the Great Fire of London. It was later rebuilt by Hawksmoor but the use of its lower quarters cost the City & South London £170,000 in compensation. It may have been an ingenious piece of engineering but it was also an expensive one. In June 1900 a second extension to Clapham Common came into use and in 1901 a further extension to Angel was opened. Moorgate was on this part of the line and there was an interchange with the Metropolitan Railway, the first example of an arrangement which became a familiar feature of the underground and indeed a necessary one, for it allowed what was basically an unplanned collection of lines to be welded into something approaching a genuine system. A northern extension to Euston was completed in 1907.

THE WATERLOO & CITY

London's second tube railway was the Waterloo & City. This was a creature of the London & South Western Railway which needed to make a quick connection from its Waterloo terminus to the City of London, the chosen destination of many of its passengers, particularly commuters. Work on building a deep level tube began in 1894 and the destination was a spot near the Mansion House, the station being called 'City' for its first forty-three years. There were two separate tunnels and electric traction was employed. The line opened on 11 July 1898. There were no intermediate stations. As an economy measure, no lifts were provided at either end of the line and passengers needed to be fairly sound in wind and limb to make it to street level. The line quickly gained the nickname 'The Drain'.

A curiosity of this line was that it has never had any physical connection with any other railway and when rolling stock needed extensive maintenance, it had, and still has, to be raised by a hoist to a connection with the main surface lines at Waterloo. Because the line was used almost exclusively by commuters, it closed early in the evening and was not open at weekends.

THE CENTRAL LONDON RAILWAY

This major undertaking was London's third tube railway. Parliamentary approval was received in August 1891 for a line six miles long from Shepherd's Bush to Cornhill in the City. This initial plan was soon altered for the route to be extended to Bank and later Liverpool Street. Work started on the building of the line in early 1896. Sir Benjamin Baker was a busy man but he found time to be the engineer-in-charge. Powerful electric locomotives were built in the USA and the coaches were more substantial than on earlier tube lines. Altogether, the 'Tuppenny Tube' as it was quickly dubbed because of its flat fare, seemed a more grown-up railway than its predecessors.

The Prince of Wales, soon to be Edward VII, performed the formal opening ceremony, as indeed he carried out several others, and the line opened to the public on 30 July 1900. Londoners (and others) thronged for an early ride. The line opened up quick and easy access from residential districts in West London through the middle of the West End and into the heart of the financial and mercantile quarter of the Metropolis. Its impact was immediately greater than that of previous tube schemes. Although it experienced teething problems, it was soon carrying heavy passenger traffic because its route enabled it to serve travellers for commuter, commercial and leisure purposes. The main problem was with the unacceptable level of vibration caused by the locomotives and it was not long before they were replaced by electric multiple-units. An ingenious innovation pioneered by the Central London Company was the placing of stations at the top of short, gentle gradients which meant that trains slowed down as they approached the stations and were able to accelerate away more quickly. This gave appreciable savings in fuel costs.

The fact that the Central London Railway was a long time gestating was partly because of various engineering problems that were encountered but largely because of the difficulty in raising the necessary capital. The sub-surface and the City & South London lines proved expensive to build but although they carried healthy numbers of passengers, they did not make much in the way of profits for their shareholders. Many other projects were able to attract smaller investors with the promise of surer and greater returns. The Central London was relatively lucky in that it managed to obtain much of its funding through a syndicate of prestigious financiers including several in the USA. Not the least of the engineering problems was persistent penetration of the workings by water from the River Tyburn, which flows under Oxford Street not far from Marble Arch and the creation of a complex subterranean underground railway interchange and system of pedestrian subways at Bank.

The Central London and indeed the other early underground lines made much in their advertising about their advantage in terms of speed over vehicular traffic on the streets above. The trains were smartly timed but they often failed to keep exactly to their schedules because of the reluctance of passengers to embark on and alight from the trains quickly enough. One journal likened the customary speed at which passengers moved to the slow and dignified progress appropriate to mourners at a funeral. This issue was a question of education and so posters and publicity urged travellers to develop the sense of urgency that was absolutely necessary if trains were to run on time. Their campaign was a successful one if the purposeful and swift movement of passengers on and off trains that we are all familiar with is anything to go by but it took a decade or more for it to become the norm.

THE UNDERGROUND AND THE GROWTH OF LONDON

The real growth of the Underground lay in the twentieth century, outside the immediate purview of this book. However the system was extending its tentacles in the late nineteenth century and playing a role in the development of London's suburbia. What helped this process was an increase in the real income and spending power of substantial numbers of the middle classes. This section of society proliferated with the large-scale expansion of the professions, of administration, commerce and the tertiary sector of the economy. Many such people were eager to live in greener, quieter surroundings away from their places of employment in Central London, much of which was still squalid, dirty and noisy. The spread of the Underground system both helped to create this demand and be a response to it.

Central London's daytime population was increasing almost exponentially while the night-time resident population declined quite dramatically. The population of the City in 1871 was 74,987. In 1901 it was just 26,923. The populations of Westminster and Holborn which were 248,363 and 93,423 respectively in 1871 fell to 183,011 and 59,405 in 1901. The daytime population of the City rose from 170,000 in 1886 to 360,000 in 1901. This meant a steady increase in commuter traffic among reasonably affluent daily travellers who could afford the fares into the leafy suburbs. The underground and suburban mainline services also benefited by the opening of substantial numbers of large department stores in Bayswater, Knightsbridge and around Oxford Street and also quality specialist shops, in Bond Street, for example. These came to be patronised on a regular basis by reasonably well-heeled suburban wives. The railways in turn helped these retail outlets. Exhibitions, theatres, galleries and other leisure activities helped to fill up seats on trains at off-peak times.

The Charing Cross Hotel in front of the South Eastern Railway's station was opened in 1865. The main line railway companies running into London vied with each other to build prestigious hotels catering for long-distance travellers.

THE UNDERGROUND AND ROAD CONGESTION

The capital's underground railways grew out of the urgent need in the middle of the nineteenth century to reduce the level of road traffic and the congestion it caused in Central London. The creation of an underground network – system seems to be the wrong word for it – was left to private enterprise without any overall strategy for the Metropolis as a whole. Did it succeed in tackling traffic congestion?

The answer is almost certainly no. The period from the 1860s to 1900 was one of almost continuous growth – of the British economy as a whole and more specifically of London's economy, of its population and of its role in the life of the nation. More and more people in the capital simply meant increased numbers moving around London travelling to and from work and for such purposes as business, pleasure and recreation. Visitors and tourists boosted the numbers on the move. Quantitative evidence is lacking. The linking of the main line termini via the emerging underground system almost certainly would have kept most travellers who arrived at one terminus and caught a train from another, off the streets. However, as has been pointed out, the main line stations generated their own road traffic in terms of hackney carriages, cabs and carts and much of this would have been of a nature unsuited to the underground.

The major public transport above ground in Central London was the horse omnibus. A division of labour seems to have taken place. In situations where underground trains and horse buses served the same districts, their relative speed over longer distances gave the trains a considerable advantage. The buses, on the other hand, were much more suitable for short journeys and very convenient with their large number of picking-up and setting-down points. This meant that buses and the underground were largely catering for the needs of different kinds of travellers. Even in the late nineteenth century there was a degree of stigma attached to bus travel and the railways astutely offered first class accommodation at premium fares for those who wouldn't have been seen dead on an omnibus. However there were tracts of Central London which in 1900 were still not served by underground trains and where, therefore, their impact on traffic congestion was minimal.

Holborn Viaduct and Queen Victoria Street were completed in 1869 and 1871 respectively by the Corporation of London as major road improvement schemes. That road congestion continued to be a bugbear of London life is evident from the radical programme of road-building launched by the London County Council in the 1890s. Among the products of this campaign were New Oxford Street, Shaftesbury Avenue, Charing Cross Road and Kingsway. They helped to tackle gridlock in the streets but they were also designed to penetrate and disperse some of Central London's most notorious slum districts and criminal rookeries such as the notorious Seven Dials and St Giles. Visitors to London throughout the nineteenth century commented on its chronic street congestion and the slowness of getting around at street level. They still do but without the railways and the Underground it would be even worse.

RAILWAYS AND SUBURBAN GROWTH

By 1900 Greater London was an almost continuously built-up area covering over fifteen miles in each direction and with a population of about six million. Suburbs were not something new to London in the nineteenth century and nor were suburbs static. It is of the nature of suburbs to start as appendages to the parent city but, if the parent grows, themselves to be absorbed by it and, in turn, to throw out their own appendages. Holborn, for example, was once a part of extramural London. It ceased to be a suburb centuries ago. Dulwich, Greenwich and Highgate were villages peripheral to London. Even when there were green fields separating them from London, they increasingly came under its influence. London crept out and gradually engulfed them and, while retaining some of their previous character, they imperceptibly changed first into suburbs and then into part of the parent 'Greater London'. This process fortunately has not totally obliterated their earlier character.

'Commuting', literally means travelling to and from work by public transport and regularly enough to earn a 'commutation' on the fare in the form of a discounted season ticket. Commuting in the broadest sense, however, if it simply means travelling a significant distance between home and work, pre-dates the railways and even horse buses. London and Westminster offered a rich variety of job opportunities and people living in outlying villages such as Islington and Camberwell would walk to and from their homes and their places of work well before Victorian times. These villages could perhaps be called 'walking suburbs'. Walking for most people was just part of living in the pre-public transport age and they thought little about regularly walking distances which would make today's devotees of sports clubs blench. Other better-off 'commuters' might use short-haul coaches and the richest would travel in their own carriages. Of course far more people lived in central London in the 1800s and being close to their work, did not need to commute. This was to change dramatically during the century. The desire to put a distance between the home and the workplace was a strong one among those Victorians who could afford it. It was an entirely understandable aspiration. London was filthy and smelly although becoming less so as the century progressed. It was overcrowded, noisy and sooty. It was also menacing.

Before the London & Greenwich Railway opened in 1836, horse buses had appeared on London's streets in 1829 with a route from Paddington to the Bank of England. Not itself a huge success, its example did, however, spawn many further routes, some of which reached out of the centre to link up with various outlying villages as well as

The first London Bridge Station.

Early semaphore signals and signal box at London Bridge.

connecting districts within central London. Competition was vigorous. This helped to keep fares down but the horse buses largely remained unaffordable to the mass of London's low paid workers as, of course, did hackney cabs.

The London & Greenwich was quickly followed by two other short lines, the London & Blackwall and the London & Croydon specifically designed to link central London with the places mentioned but after that much of London's rapidly growing railway network consisted of longer lines even if they were not of the inter-city character of, say, the London & Birmingham or the London & Southampton. An example was the North Kent Railway opened in 1849 and running out via Lewisham, Blackheath and Woolwich to the Medway towns. Lewisham and Blackheath were already highly desirable residential villages with many large houses. Lewisham began to take on a much more working-class character after the railway was built. Blackheath continued to be fashionable although enclaves of working-class housing developed, some of their residents finding work locally, in the big houses for example, and others commuting the short distance to London Bridge. Horse buses appeared, feeding passengers onto the railway at Blackheath from neighbouring, still very rural, villages such as Eltham.

The first underground railway ran from Paddington to Farringdon and opened in 1863. It was designed to alleviate the appalling traffic congestion that had built up along

Cannon Street Station. This was opened in 1866 by the SER to gain access to the City.

Cannon Street Station as seen from the Thames. It was far more impressive when it had its overall roof than the dreary nondescript building that can be seen today.

the New Road (now the Euston and Marylebone Roads) which ironically was itself a by-pass designed to tackle overcrowded road conditions in the centre of London. It was not the immediate stunning success that had been hoped for but in the longer term it was a model for the building of a network of sub-surface and tube lines which have proved to be vital transport arteries, not least for carrying commuters to and from the suburbs.

In the 1870s a new form of public transport began to appear on London's streets or in particular parts of them. This was the horse tram. The use of rails enabled horses to pull a car with a bigger potential payload than a horse bus. The horse trams were the archetypal working class form of transport. They charged much cheaper fares than the railways and although they were slower they had the convenience of running more frequently and calling at far more stops. A network of routes run by different companies developed mainly serving areas of working class housing in the inner suburbs. They were largely excluded from central London but the railways quickly found that the horse trams and especially their electric successors provided serious competition in the inner suburbs. Where the trams passed through undeveloped districts, housing soon followed and a senior official of one of the tramway companies was able to say that in 1884 his trams had helped to relieve overcrowding in the centre of London by making it possible for working class people to live a few miles out and commute. A knock-on effect was that in some of the inner suburbs, the previous inhabitants who liked to think of themselves as genteel, moved further out of London as more proletarian neighbours moved in.

It has already been mentioned that many of the railway companies had little initial interest in providing services at the lower end of the market. The Great Western Railway even staunchly refused to use the word 'suburban' in its timetables well into the 1860s. Such an attitude was only one of the many ways in which the railway companies attracted public criticism. Events were to force their hand. The North London Railway was the first company to be required by Parliament to make some provision for those made homeless by the building of a new line. A great deal of demolition was involved when their Broad Street terminus was built in the middle of the 1860s and they had to agree to put on special workmen's trains with low fares. The Great Eastern had to pay the same price a few years later when contemplating building its Liverpool Street terminus next door to Broad Street. In 1883 a Cheap Trains Act was passed which in most cases insisted that railway companies ran special trains with cheap fares for working people. Workmen's tickets proved a great boon when they became generally available for those travelling before a certain time in the morning. Even then, there were considerable differences between the fares charged by different companies.

Not everyone was pleased with the workmen's fares. They had the same kind of effect on middle-class suburbs that the horse trams had. They brought the tone down! The middle-class residents of such suburbs as Stamford Hill, Tottenham and Edmonton were appalled when their tranquil existence was threatened by proletarians taking up residence in their neighbourhood, attracted by cheap fares on the Great Eastern Railway. The *petit bourgeoisie* moved on to pastures new.

A workman's train.

It would be too easy to say that all the railways did was to encourage a kind of decanting process as people tended to move out of central London and that each suburb took on a distinctive class character with the better-off constantly moving further out. The reality was far more complex. The population of Greater London grew rapidly but certain districts grew far faster than others. The headlong growth of West Ham has already been mentioned. The newcomers to London had frequently migrated from the provinces or from further afield in the British Isles and they did not necessarily want to live in central London. While their job prospects and earning expectations had a considerable bearing on what they could afford in the way of housing, they might not be looking to live and work in the centre. As suburbs became established, they took on an economic life of their own. Some became towns in their own right, being both urban and suburban, dependent it is true on being near London but with a wide range of employment opportunities of their own. Wealthy suburbs needed hordes of domestic servants who were not well-paid and who therefore tended to live fairly close to their work. Most suburbs took on a mixed character and a former village like Hampstead which was already fashionable before the railways arrived and continued to be fashionable, developed pockets of deprivation almost cheek-by-jowl with others of conspicuous wealth.

The London & Southampton Railway (later to be the London & South Western) had its first London terminus at Nine Elms, Battersea. The line opened in 1838 and stations were provided in the westerly direction at Wandsworth, Wimbledon and 'Kingston'. The history of stations with anomalous names is a rich and fascinating one and Kingston might qualify for inclusion. It was a short distance from the ancient and important town of Kingston-on-Thames. Kingston was an obvious and convenient hook on which to hang a name that it was hoped would attract business. An affluent settlement developed around the station which came to be known in some quarters as 'Kingston-on-Railway'. Such a prosaic name was not really a misnomer but it displeased the well-to-do incomers and so, miraculously, 'Surbiton', an old name for the neighbourhood, was revived, dusted down and bestowed on what it was hoped would continue to be a socially exclusive neighbourhood graced by a railway which could carry the paterfamilias quickly and easily to and from his workplace in Westminster or the City. Surbiton proved to be a lusty infant, resenting and for generations succeeding in fighting off every attempt by its larger neighbour, Kingston-on-Thames, to subsume it. It has been described by that great railway historian, Professor Jack Simmons as '...the oldest suburb in Europe, perhaps in the world, that was called into being by a railway'.

Croydon, with a population of about 12,500 in the 1830s, was a substantial town before the railways arrived. Being on the main road from London to Brighton, it was busy with stagecoaches in which some people commuted to London. It became an important focal point for railways which contributed to its very rapid growth, especially in the 1860s. It came to enjoy fast and frequent services to London with no fewer than eight stations within its purlieus and it gained a character both urban in its own right and suburban because it was the favoured dormitory of very large numbers of commuters. It had pockets of real affluence in the nineteenth century but never the exclusivity that the inhabitants of Surbiton fought so valorously to preserve. A large network of short-distance surface railways played a major role in opening up access to the countryside of Kent and Surrey and contributed much to the extension of Greater London into those areas. 'Southern Electric' became a familiar slogan in the twentieth century.

It is a truism and the source of much banter that London north of the river is very different from those parts of the metropolis to the south of the Thames. Historically, it is undeniable that in terms of population and many other factors, the centre of gravity of ancient London was located north of the Thames around the City and Westminster. A substantial and important transport line suburb did however develop around Southwark and the Borough in which the station at London Bridge was to become a major feature. The railways north of the river were very different from those to the south. Four major companies, or a fifth you include the Great Central with its belated arrival on the scene, ran out of London in a northern or westerly direction. They were the Great Western, Great Central, London & North Western, Midland and Great Northern operating out of Paddington, Marylebone, Euston, St Pancras and King's Cross respectively. Leaving the Great Central aside, the other four companies were interested mainly in long-distance traffic at least at first and the few stations that were open in the early years within twenty miles of London had infrequent services.

The GWR opened a station at Ealing in 1838. The village was small but an established and affluent one with many large houses and traffic was slow to develop at first. In conjunction with the Metropolitan Railway a limited service of through carriages from Ealing was put on running into the City. In the 1860s and 1870s with large-scale residential development taking place, railway business at Ealing grew rapidly. From 1879 the GWR found itself in competition with the District Railway whose avowed intention was to encourage house building along its line from central London via Hammersmith. It had some success. The GWR now responded by putting on through trains to the City but the District Railway seized much of the growing commuter traffic because its line provided access to a wider range of places in central London. In the 1890s, Ealing was sometimes referred to as the 'Queen of the Western Suburbs' having grown large relatively gracefully. What working-class housing existed was mostly tucked away in West Ealing and was very much a feature of its south-eastern neighbour, Acton. Modern Ealing would not be what it is without the railway.

The LNWR was not initially interested in local services out of Euston and it was almost by chance that what became Willesden Junction developed into a major interchange with the North London Railway. Several long-distance expresses called there because the North London Railway provided handy connections with many parts of Greater London. Housing development took place around Willesden but the fate of the surrounding area was largely dictated by the many lines that converged at Willesden and its near-neighbour Old Oak Common. They became the centre of a tangle of engine sheds, carriage sidings, shunting yards and industrial development, much of the latter there because of the railways.

The Midland Railway showed little interest at first in local traffic into and out of St Pancras, except perhaps at Hendon but it did build the Tottenham and Hampstead line, jointly with the Great Eastern Railway, largely so it could get access to the London Docks and keep other companies out. There were a number of stations along the line but little evidence that its presence contributed to the residential development of the districts through which it passed. The Great Northern, by contrast saw the possibilities for traffic in the Northern Heights and beyond and extruded a line from Finsbury Park north-westwards to the then rural fastnesses of High Barnet and Mill Hill with a branch from Highgate to Alexandra Palace. Another branch left the main line at Wood Green

GREAT NORTHERN RAILWAY.

On and after the 1st July,

A NEW STATION

WILL BE

OPENED

AT

SEVEN SISTERS' ROAD,

HOLLOWAY,

At which Passenger Trains will call as under:

DOWN.	WEEK DAYS.		SUNDAYS.

	morn	morn.	Saturday only morn. after.	after.	after.	after.	after.	morn.	morn.	after.	after.
King's Cross ...dep.	6.00,	9.05,	11.20,	3.0,	5.10,	6.5,	7.0,	9.20	7.30,	9.0,	5.20,	6.0

UP.											
	morn.	morn.	morn.	after.	after.	after.	after.	morn.	after.	after.	
Seven Sisters' Road ..dep.	8.20,	9.18,	11.25,	1.20,	5.20,	7.15,	8.41	9.35,	8.28,	8.55	

Fares between King's Cross and Seven Sisters' Road Stations.

SINGLE.			RETURN.	
1st Class.	2nd Class	3rd Class.	1st Class.	2nd Class.
7d.	**4d.**	**2½d.**	**10d.**	**6d.**

SEASON TICKETS.

	3 months.	4 mon.	6 mon	7 mon	8 mon	9 mon.	10 mon.	11 mon.	12 mon.
1st Class ...	£2 9 0	£3 3 0	£3 16 0	£4 7 6	£4 18	£5 7 6	£5 15 6	£6 2 6	£6 11 6 £7 0 0
2nd Class...	1 11 6	2 0 6	2 8 9	2 16 3	3 3	3 9 0	3 14 3	3 18 9	4 4 6 4 10

No Goods or Coal business will be conducted at Seven Sisters' Station.

By order,   SEYMOUR CLARKE,

London, King's Cross Station, 28th June, 1861.   General Manager.

Waterlow and Sons, Printers, Carpenters' Hall, London Wall.

A Great Northern Railway handbill for the opening of a new station at Seven Sisters Road. The station opened on 1 July 1861 in what was a largely rural district. It is now the heaving transport hub of Finsbury Park.

and headed for Enfield. These schemes with the exception of the Alexandra Palace line were carried out partly for imperialistic reasons to pre-empt other companies moving in or to provide competition and give them a run for their money. Opened in the late 1860s and early 1870s, with the exception of the 'Ally Pally' branch, they were mostly successful in attracting residential development and generating passenger usage.

As London grew from the Middle Ages through to the eighteenth century, new building development tended to take place to the west of the City. A feature of the nineteenth century, however, was London's growth eastwards and the railways played an important role in this. A few well-to-do carriage folk had large houses in such places as Hackney, Clapton and Enfield but the Lea Valley, marshy and bleak, was a deterrent to systematic building development.

It is likely that the London & Blackwall Railway helped to stimulate the growth of places like Limehouse and Poplar but the most obvious development was that stimulated by the Eastern Counties (from 1862 the Great Eastern) Railway along its line towards Cambridge following the Lea Valley, opened in 1840. The Eastern Counties wanted short-haul passenger traffic and opened up numerous stations on this route as far as Broxbourne and threw off branch lines to Enfield (1849) and to Loughton in 1856.

The Eastern Counties Railway was a standing joke for tardiness and inefficiency but among its meagre successes was that in the Lea Valley. This had been noticed and the consequence of this was that the Great Eastern as it now was found landowners in the still rural areas to the north-east of London eager to sell their land for building development so long as railways provided the necessary transport infrastructure. The results of this opportunism were a line to Walthamstow opened in 1870, extended to Chingford in 1873 and another through Stoke Newington to Edmonton opened in 1872. Large-scale housing development followed these lines with strict social segregation. The sections from London to Walthamstow and Edmonton through places such as Tottenham and Clapton saw housing built predominantly for artisans, shop-workers and clerks. They were crammed into uniform terraces with the tiniest gardens front and rear and built to the minimum standards laid down by the Public Health Act of 1875. The stations in these districts were provided with large numbers of workmen's trains while, by contrast, beyond Walthamstow to Chingford the higher and healthier country away from the Lea Valley attracted a much more middle-class population.

The Great Eastern was a victim of its own success, generating so much traffic to and from the inner working-class suburbs as to put a severe strain on line capacity. Indeed the Great Eastern found itself operating what was said to be the most intensive steam-hauled local passenger services in the world and it is only fair to add that it performed miracles with the diminutive locomotives of the early years heaving heavy loads up Bethnal Green Bank. Having both the pleasure and the pain resulting from its role in creating the working-class suburbs with their high levels of passenger usage, they reined back and refused to issue workmen's tickets from stations beyond Walthamstow and on the Loughton branch, thus engaging in a piece of social engineering, effectively deterring builders from erecting homes for working class people. So while Walthamstow's population developed from 5,000 in 1851 to nearly 100,000 in 1901, other small towns like Loughton, Chingford and Epping remained socially more exclusive and therefore did not expand at anything like the same rate.

An old coach of the Eastern Counties Railway. The derivation of this Spartan vehicle from a stage coach is fairly obvious.

The London County Council, established in the late 1880s, did all it could to encourage cheap workmen's fares. Many people who could by no means be described as 'workmen' took advantage of the cheap fares which often meant an extremely early journey into London. In many cases such as the Great Eastern Railway it also involved travelling in cramped and uncomfortable rolling stock on the basis, presumably, of the passenger getting what he paid for. The railway companies were evasive on the issue of whether they made profits on shifting the commuters travelling with such tickets. They certainly shifted them in huge quantities but in doing so incurred the wasteful expense of utilising rolling stock which at worst might only make one inward and one outward journey per day. The railway companies' real interest was in the much more lucrative business of serving the needs of first and second class passengers. They were very successful in making railway travel the accepted way in which the middle class suburbanites not only went to and fro from work but used also them for socialising and other leisure purposes.

The London, Tilbury & Southend Railway was opened in the 1850s primarily to serve what was thought would be a lucrative potential excursion traffic at Southend and later in the 1880s freight traffic to the developing docks at Tilbury. A second line further north through Upminster was opened in 1885. The western end of the line was soon carrying an intensive cheap suburban traffic from such places as Barking and Plaistow which developed very rapidly as residential districts for the working-class. The LTSR proved to be the most prosperous of all the railways serving the inner suburbs and its

All the early railway companies proudly wanted their own distinctive 'image'. Rolling stock was painted in distinctive liveries and some companies reproduced their seal on carriages. This example is from the London, Tilbury & Southend Railway.

growth was positively headlong. In 1870-4 the average number of passengers carried annually was 1,939,082. In the first decade of the twentieth century the figure reached over 3 million.

If it had been possible, most builders would have preferred to erect housing for middle-class occupants. Ideally they wanted stations to have fast and frequent services up to town and the stations to be located less than a mile from the housing developments. The speculative builders wanted land to be available at prices they thought reasonable and in places which met the other criteria. All this was at best an elusive mix and some developers got their fingers badly burnt. Some bought land only to find that various factors beyond their control might make it impossible for them to proceed with their plans which left them watching the value of their investment evaporate.

It was not just the builders who took a risk and sometimes came unstuck. A railway company might build a line through a rural and sparsely-populated locality in London's hinterland in the confident expectation that the opening of stations would attract builders and rapid housing development. One oft-quoted example of such a line which was an almost total failure in this respect was the Great Eastern Railway's Edmonton to Cheshunt Loop. This was opened in 1891 and provided with three intermediate stations. There was however, as it proved, nothing automatic about housing following the opening of a railway. It simply did not happen with this line which had the dubious distinction in 1909 of being among the first in the Greater London area to close to passenger traffic. It was of course successfully reopened in 1960.

Summing up, the railways were a necessary but not of themselves a sufficient condition for the growth of many of London's inner and outer suburbs. Even today for those who care to look, a journey on a local train out of many of London's termini can provide fascinating visual evidence of the layer cake nature of Victorian housing development and support for both the specific and the general points made in this chapter. It can also provide evidence that contradicts those points. That is the fascination of history and the fascination of London.

RAILWAYS AND THE PURSUIT OF PLEASURE

TRIPS OUT

It was of the nature of life that Londoners worked hard and played hard. Some of the local nineteenth century attractions waiting for their halfpennies and pennies were commercial businesses like Cremorne Gardens, Chelsea and Vauxhall Gardens; Beulah Spa at Dulwich; Bermondsey Spa also south of the river and Bagnigge Wells and Islington Spa at Finsbury. Changing fashions in the nineteenth century were not kind to such ventures and they went into decline. However, London has always had the advantage of possessing numerous historic open spaces, many of them openly accessible for the public. These were added to by such gems as Victoria Park in 1842. Many historic villages, woods and open spaces drew the masses on high days and holidays and although the places themselves were free, they gathered various attractions and amenities which could be had for a few pence. Trips up and down the Thames, increasingly during the nineteenth century by steamboat, were immensely popular. London's rising population and its growing aggregate wealth and spending power made the commercial provision of leisure sound financial sense.

It was inevitable that the railways would get in on the act. The London & Greenwich was one of the first companies to react to what it perceived as a potential demand and it started running an intensive service on Sundays at very cheap fares which allowed people to leave Greenwich to return to central London after midnight. Other companies such as the London, Brighton & South Coast Railway took the idea up in the 1840s and ran extremely cheap excursions from London to Brighton on Sundays. These proved exceptionally popular and the arrival of trainloads of chirpy, cheerful Cockneys added another facet to the already many-sided character of Brighton. It was not long before claims were being made that increased crime in the town could be blamed on outsiders, especially trippers from London.

An unofficial estimate on one Sunday in 1857 suggested that about 42,000 pleasure-seekers had left six London terminus stations on special trains with discounted fares. The gay abandon and single-minded hedonism of the trippers, the avarice of the railway companies determined to make money and the individual greed of those workers involved in running the excursions on a Sunday incurred the wrath of the Sabbatarian movement and in particular the Lord's Day Observance Society. They did not want the sanctity of what they regarded as the Sabbath to be profaned by levity and licentiousness.

Instead they thought that Sundays should be given over to attendance at worship and to rest and quiet contemplation. Dire warnings were gleefully issued of the hellish condign fate awaiting those foolish enough to make such outings but they fell on deaf ears. The vast majority of workers had no truck with such arguments. Sunday was their one day off work and by hook or by crook, it was to be enjoyed. Their desire for pleasure and the commercial considerations of the railway companies and the interests of the business communities in the places the excursion trains visited ensured that Sunday specials had arrived and would stay. It has to be said, however, that there were still large numbers of Londoners in low-paid, periodic or partial employment for whom the cost of such travel was simply impossible, even at the end of the century.

Most people in trade and commerce worked on Saturdays in the first half of the nineteenth century. Shop-workers gradually won the right to a half-day with early closing on a day in the middle of the week. Pressure developed from the 1840s through organisations such as the Early Closing Association for Saturdays to be worked as a half-day. The Association did not advocate that the extra few hours away from work should be spent asleep or getting drunk in the pub. It was keen on the idea that workers and their families should get out into the countryside enjoying a commune with nature and filling their lungs with air that was inevitable cleaner than that in Central London. Perhaps they could learn to recognise a few wild flowers or the call of some songbirds. It was believed that they would benefit immensely from this form of 'rational recreation'. What better form of transport was there than the railway to carry them out to the babbling brooks, the meandering lanes and the ancient churches embowered in yews and rook-infested sturdy old oaks?

One of the first substantial employers to give their workers Saturday afternoon off was Truman, Hanbury & Buxton, the brewers of Shoreditch. The move to close workplaces around midday was a drawn-out process but had two results in railway terms. The first was for extra trains to deal with the flow of homeward-bound workers after midday. Second was the appearance of regular timetabled Saturdays-only half-day excursions to various destinations from London stations on Saturday afternoons. The first of these seems to have run on the South Eastern & Chatham Railway in 1857 and enabled its users to enjoy the delights of Woolwich or Blackheath while not having to return from those places until as late as ten o' clock. By 1887 no fewer than 115 such Saturdays-only trains were leaving London.

The Victorian period was one of slowly-rising living standards and expectations for a substantial section of the population. Although there were occasional setbacks in the form of slumps or banking crises, generally from the mid-1840s the economy was expanding with growing employment opportunities. Especially with the price of some foodstuffs falling significantly towards the end of the century, large numbers of lower middle-class and skilled and semi-skilled workers in regular employment were enjoying rising real wages. More money to spend combined with some decline in working hours created a demand for packaged, commercialised leisure provision. For that substantial underbelly of the London working-class living in poverty and who were trapped in casual jobs, the sweated industries or frequently in and out of employment, the benefits of travelling out of Town to the seaside or to some place of beauty or historical interest largely remained elusive.

Evidence of the heightened aspirations of some middle and working-class Londoners was the issuing of cheap tickets to a seaside or other destination for travel outward on Saturday with a return on Sunday or even Monday. Thus was born the week-end holiday. The first such tickets were advertised in the 1840s and they must eventually have generated useful business because a few companies ran Mondays-only return trains from such places as Felixstowe, Ramsgate and Bournemouth.

Of course travelling to and staying by the sea was not feasible for the bulk of working-class Londoners who had to be content with something closer to home. London was well-placed in that respect with natural attractions and beauty spots in all directions. Epping Forest had long been a well-loved destination and became much easier to reach once the railway line to Chingford opened in 1873. A good warm sunny Sunday could see the Forest besieged by at least 50,000 Londoners, the bulk of them from the East End. Other favourite resorts were Blackheath, Greenwich, Hampstead, Kew Gardens, Richmond and Wimbledon all of which were readily accessible by rail by 1870 or earlier. Another series of places easily accessible by rail if further away were Hampton Court, Windsor and the North Downs around Dorking. There were many others. A couple of enterprising companies even put on anglers' tickets at a discounted rate while ramblers could have tickets which allowed them to travel out of London on one line and return on another. The railways helped people to escape the sounds and smells of London, even if only temporarily. In 1853 a senior City of London police officer declared that the streets of the City were almost deserted on warm sunny Sundays as the locals had used the trains to get out into the countryside for picnics and rambles.

RAILWAYS AND SPORT

Railways were an important influence on the siting of a number of professional football grounds. Extremely rough and ready games with few rules and many injuries had been played since time immemorial. In the nineteenth century such activities increasingly found themselves under critical scrutiny. Large gatherings of working people, especially young men, were boisterous, often drunken and came to be regarded as a potential threat to law and order. The physical energy and passions that such games aroused needed to be channelled and controlled. The second half of the nineteenth century saw the emergence of national bodies that codified the game with rules and discipline at all levels including the novel concept that players would obey a referee – the impartial man in charge and arbiter of disputes. The bigger clubs began to build enclosed stadiums and they went down the road of commercialisation and professionalism. With serious amounts of money being invested in clubs, it was important to attract paying spectators in large numbers. The football grounds therefore had to be readily accessible and railways were seen as an ideal way of shifting the large crowds making their way to and from the matches.

Tottenham Hotspur had their first enclosed ground at Northumberland Park in 1888 but it proved too small for the club's ambitions. They then built a new state-of-the-art stadium in Tottenham intentionally close to the White Hart Lane station of the Great Eastern Railway. Proximity to railways was very much a factor in the siting of Chelsea's Stamford Bridge ground and Queen's Park Rangers even had a ground built for them by the Great Western Railway. The Den, the former ground of Millwall, was located close to three railway stations and one of Fulham's early grounds was near Parsons Green

One of a series of prints of 1845 showing batting strokes. This one is called 'Leg half-Volley' and is a shot rarely seen except perhaps on the village green. Railways did much to encourage the development of the higher levels of cricket as a spectator sport.

underground station. The Crystal Palace was the venue for a number of cup finals in the late 1890s and early 1900s. It was well-served by railways, the two stations catering for that popular venue being large and designed for the shifting of big crowds.

Just as anarchic violent football attracted the opprobrium of the middle classes, so prize-fighting or pugilism also drew down their disapproval. It was barbaric, the contestants sometimes receiving appalling injuries which on occasions proved fatal; the crowd becoming frenziedly excited because of the amount involved in the bets being laid on the outcome while fights broke out among the partisan and frequently drunk spectators. Huge crowds attended bouts between the best-known fighters and they even included roués from the aristocratic classes. Increasingly magistrates banned such bouts and they were driven 'underground'. When and where possible, locations were found in natural hollows, preferably in remote spots near country railway stations. It was even better if such locations were close to a county border so that in the event of a raid, all concerned could slip 'next door' into an area of different police jurisdiction. The railway companies had no scruples about organising special trains to what at best were semi-legal events. The destinations were kept secret to the last minute and it is even said that when the footplate crew and guard reported for duty, they had no idea where their destination would be that day although of course the driver had to 'sign the road', that is, have the necessary route knowledge. Examples of excursion trains being put on for London devotees of pugilism were those to Sawbridgeworth in 1842 by the Northern

& Eastern Railway, Wolverton in 1845 (the London & Birmingham) and the London & South Western to Farnborough in Hampshire in 1860.

Samuel Smiles, the very model of mid-Victorian earnestness, would be expected to have been supportive of railway excursions to places of historical interest or natural beauty as part of the concept of 'rational recreation'. He occupied the position of Secretary to the South Eastern Railway and in 1859 he had to appear before a hostile committee appointed by the Home Office to explain why his company persisted in running excursions to prize-fights. He was disarmingly candid. He told them that demand and the prospect of profit made the opportunity to put these trains on absolutely irresistible. Commercial considerations took precedence over ethics.

Railways made a considerable contribution to the development of horse-racing, the so called 'Sport of Kings'. Like football, horse-racing became codified and controlled in the nineteenth century and, similarly, the venues at which the sport took place were now being enclosed and becoming far more commercialised. With large amounts of capital invested in the industry, it became important to draw in the crowds. The railways and the horse-racing industry marched forward together, mutually supportive. The southern environs of London had several race courses which with one exception were handily served by rail. The best-known course was probably Epsom and this was served first of all by the London, Brighton & South Coast Railway's Epsom Downs Station opened in 1865 followed by the South Eastern & Chatham with Tattenham Corner Station in

'Aldine' winning the Goodwood Stakes in 1853. The growth of the horse-racing industry owed much to the railway companies who were able to move large numbers of paying spectators to the course which were sometimes deep in the countryside.

1901. Remarkably, these were the termini of lines specially-built to serve the racecourse and which saw minimal use other then on the few race days per annum. At their outer ends these lines both traversed largely empty countryside but both stations were large. Epsom Downs had eight platforms and Tattenham Corner had six and such was their usage on race days that even these generous facilities were fully stretched. Further away were other racecourses such as Newmarket, Doncaster and Aintree, all of which were served by special trains from London. In 1905 a course was opened at Newbury. The GWR had a financial interest in this project and built a station, only open on race days, adjacent to its Reading to Taunton main line. Trains ran directly to it from Paddington.

THE DISTRICT RAILWAY AND EXHIBITIONS

The Victorian era was one of belief in the infinite potential for progress of which mankind was capable. There was an intense belief in the harnessing of the arts, science and technology in order to create a better world. There was a sense of awe and wonderment about a planet which was shrinking with the development of new and faster forms of communications such as steamships, railways and the electric telegraph. There was a thirst for knowledge and self-improvement. It is hardly surprising therefore that the nineteenth century saw the staging of a large number of exhibitions, especially in London. Railways played a crucial part in making these events possible by providing the visitors with the means of transport for getting there and back.

The District Railway benefited by being able to serve the area sometimes known as 'Albertopolis' or 'Museumland'. Prince Albert had invested much time and effort in the planning of the Great Exhibition of 1851. He was a very serious man and he very earnestly, if somewhat naively, believed that the development of international trading links was a path to international amity and that this worthy concept would be encouraged by an exhibition that brought together the industrial and commercial products of the developed and developing nations and emphasised the intertwining of art and manufacture. The Great Exhibition was a marked success (even if it was distinctly nationalistic) and the profits from it partly went to the buying of land and the building of museums and educational establishments in what became the Exhibition Road area of South Kensington. The station at South Kensington which came to be served by trains of the District and Circle Lines was opened in 1868. It was ideally placed to bring visitors to the various attractions of this cultural quarter. A pedestrian tunnel twenty-two chains long was opened in 1885 to allow underground passengers for free and non-railway users for a toll of a penny to walk under cover from South Kensington to the cluster of attractions around Exhibition Road. The first exhibition to be served by the District Railway was the International Inventions Exhibition in 1871.

The Earl's Court as a place for exhibitions opened in 1887 on a patch of derelict land between various railway lines and very close to the District Line's West Brompton Station as well as Earl's Court Station itself. The District opened a covered pedestrian way from the station to Warwick Road and the entrance to the exhibition ground. Over the next few years many successful exhibitions and other spectacles were staged at Earl's Court and the District did good business taking people to and fro. An excellent earner for the District was the Big Wheel which was a prominent feature of the West London skyline from 1895 to 1906.

The National Agricultural Hall was yet another exhibition centre to open up in this district. It started business in 1884 and was renamed 'Olympia' in 1886. It came to be known for spectacular shows which combined education and entertainment. The exhibition centre was next to Addison Road Station (now Kensington Olympia) which, although it was not served directly by District Line trains, brought the company revenue from originating stations on its own lines.

In the ways mentioned and by many other means, railways played a critical role in the development of leisure for the teeming millions of London.

THE SUPPLY OF COAL AND FOOD TO LONDON

Black Gold

Traditionally, London's coal was brought down the east coast in tough little collier ships from the Tyne and the Wear. Their virtual monopoly and its effect on the price of coal was a long-standing source of resentment. An additional irritation was because the coasting trade was sometimes affected by inclement weather, preventing the movement of the seacoal and causing shortages in the capital accompanied by sharp price rises. High hopes were voiced early on that the railways might be able to break this monopoly, leading to a substantial fall in the price of coal in the capital. This consideration was undoubtedly a factor in the minds of the promoters of the Stockton & Darlington Railway whose line was designed to move coal from pits in County Durham to the River Tees. From the Tees it could be shipped down the coast to London, hopefully undercutting the coal from further north.

In the event the railways were slow off the mark so far as carrying coals to London was concerned. It seems that the first regular bulk consignments of coal to London began in 1845, travelling a rather circuitous route from Derbyshire via Rugby, originating on the Midland Railway and running into London over the metals of the LNWR. In 1850, 55,000 tons of rail-borne coal arrived in London as opposed to the 3.5 million tons that arrived by sea. After that time, however, the railways became seriously interested in the financial potential of carrying coal to London to supply the immense and growing demand from industrial and domestic consumers. The Great Northern Railway was the first company to enter this business seriously and soon after its direct line from Doncaster via Grantham and Peterborough opened in 1850, it began shifting trainloads of coal from South Yorkshire and the East Midlands. The London & North Western Railway was not far behind. In 1867 rail-borne coal exceeded that carried by sea for the first time. The coastal trade fought a rearguard action with bigger ships and better loading and unloading methods but the railways maintained their domination of the traffic. The Midland Railway entered the trade in a serious way after its own direct line to London was opened, competing most directly with the GNR while the Great Western Railway also supplied the London market with particularly high quality types of coal from South Wales. The Midland Railway went on to become the largest mover of coal to London.

Nearly all of London's rail-borne coal arrived at yards in the north and west of the metropolis but there was of course considerable demand for coal from places south of the Thames. The trains of coal were sorted in large marshalling yards such as Brent (Midland Railway) and Ferme Park (GNR) in North London and then tripped around London via the West London/ West London Extension Line or through Central London via the Metropolitan Railway and then over the line of the LC& DR through Ludgate Hill to depots in South London. The LNWR for example had a coal depot at Tulse Hill and even a joint one with its hated rival, the Midland Railway, at Peckham Rye, opened in 1891. An example of enterprise was the LNWR's agreement with the North London Railway which enabled it not only to have access to the London Docks but also to elevated coal depots at Broad Street and Haggerston and to sidings in such places as Kingsland, Hackney, Bow and Poplar and to various industries in the East End that needed large and regular supplies of coal. A sizeable yard was built at Hither Green in the 1890s just to the south-east of Lewisham which handled large amounts of coal brought in by Great Northern and Midland Railway trains. These had travelled over the Metropolitan, the LC & DR and a link from Blackfriars Junction to Metropolitan Junction on the South Eastern Railway, opened in 1878.

The coal which arrived from the provinces in train loads was sorted into local pick-up goods trains which dropped off three or four loaded wagons here and half-a-dozen there. Almost every station in London's periphery eventually had two or three coal sidings with their characteristic storage bunkers made of old sleepers, rows of carts, coal merchants' offices and weighbridges. The coal was sacked up and then delivered to the domestic consumer by horse and cart. Larger industrial premises might have their own coal sidings. The railway wagons themselves were of small capacity and wooden-bodied and were either owned by the colliery companies or by coal merchants. In either case, the names were prominently displayed on the sides. Where space was limited, coal drops were built so that coal could be discharged from wagons directly into bunkers below.

During the nineteenth century, the amount of seaborne coal arriving in London continued to increase but the railways' share of the growing trade grew much more quickly to something like 60% in the 1880s. The railways played the major role in keeping the capital reliably supplied with coal at affordable prices. Coal was the source of Victorian London's lighting and heating. The railways therefore performed a task of vital importance to the capital's development.

BRINGING IN THE MEAT

Londoners hungered for meat; the demand for it was immense. The railways contributed to satisfying that demand.

There were four wholesale meat markets in or close to the City. The major one was Smithfield. It was also the most contentious. It had been established in 1638 by the City of London Corporation and quickly attracted criticism because of the mess made in the streets by animals being driven there. The drovers were notorious for their drunken and offensive behaviour. The animals often got out of control and charged around the streets, causing mayhem and injury. The beasts were slaughtered at premises around the market and the sight and sound of this was becoming increasingly offensive and unacceptable by the nineteenth century. Blood and reeking heaps of gore piled up in the surrounding streets. In 1855 the market in live meat was transferred to a new site at Copenhagen Fields, north of King's Cross. The Metropolitan Cattle Market had no direct railway link but was close to the Great Northern Railway. The old Smithfield was then rebuilt as the main London market for dead meat. It was adjacent to the Metropolitan Railway and the Great Western Railway opened a subterranean depot into which whole trains could be shunted. It never really caught on.

The London & North Western and the Great Western developed a sophisticated business moving imported cattle from Ireland, often slaughtered where the beasts came into England, for example at Birkenhead, and much of this ended up on the London market. Through the century, an increasing amount of dead meat came into Britain from overseas. In 1872 a Foreign Cattle Market opened at Deptford on the Thames and it was served by a branch of the London, Brighton and South Coast Railway. The development of refrigeration meant that large and fast ships crossed the world from countries like Argentina, Australia and New Zealand and were able to bring substantial supplies of cheap frozen meat into the London Docks. The capital took the lion's share of this meat but the railway companies with the GWR and the Midland most dominant, were at the forefront of developing refrigerated vans which then distributed meat around the country.

THE FLYING KIPPER

The Revd W. Awdry had a 'Flying Kipper' express fish train in one of his marvellous railway stories for children. In fact kippers, being smoked and cured, were not in need of especially rapid transportation and along with dried, salted fish, had for centuries been sent by sea down the east coast and up the Thames to London. They formed a significant but probably not particularly popular part of the diet of Londoners, useful especially at times when meat was scarce or, at least in theory, banned for religious reasons. For centuries fresh fish had been caught off the coasts of Kent and Essex and landed for the London market at Queenhithe and Billingsgate. Fresh fish were also taken from the Thames itself and coarse fish from some of its tributaries in the London area and from ponds and other watercourses. However, Londoners had the reputation of not being particularly keen on eating fish. Sprats, whitebait and jellied eels were exceptions to the rule.

This situation changed rapidly in the Victorian period as the railways developed an extensive business in carrying fresh fish, a highly perishable commodity which benefited by the speed the companies could offer in getting it in reasonable condition to the London market. An argument could be put forward to the effect that Grimsby, Lowestoft or Fleetwood, for example, were every bit as much railway towns as the better-known Crewe, Swindon or Eastleigh. The railways were the making of these fishing ports leading to the development of a large-scale, highly capitalised industry dependent on rail for whisking the precious and perishable cargo off to the urban markets, especially London. This is not the place to enter into the avid and emotional debates as to whether fish was first fried with chipped potatoes in London or in any one of a number of locations in the north of England. Wherever fish and chips was

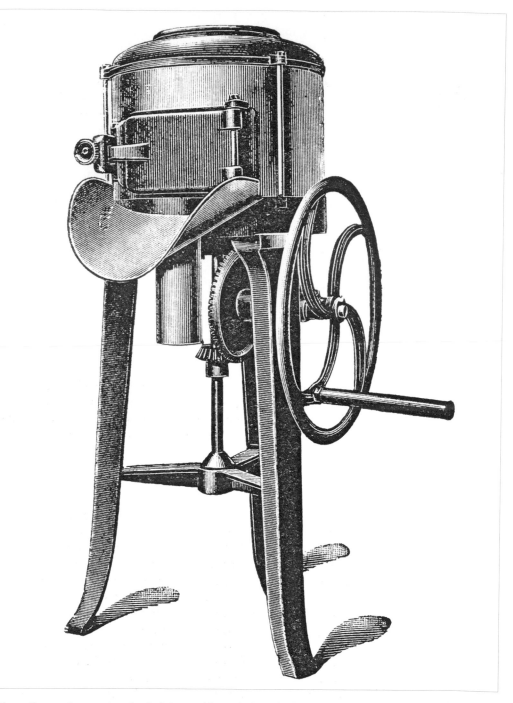

The railways, by moving fresh fish quickly and cheaply from port to market, did much to assist the growth of that most traditional of English dishes, fish and chips. In turn an industry developed providing the apparatus, utensils and accessories needed by the fish fryer.

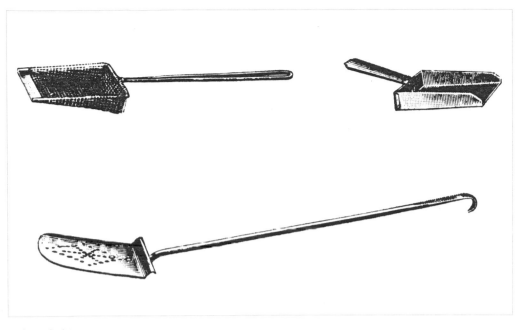

Fish and chip scoops.

invented, with the aid of the railways it became a staple item of the diet of working-class Londoners. It was cheap, it was sustaining and it was responsible for bringing about a very marked improvement in the diet and the health of the working class. The middle-class, however, affected to look down on fish and chips. That was their loss.

FRUIT AND VEG

London, because of the size of its population, had for centuries exerted a strong influence on the agricultural and horticultural activities which took place in the rural hinterland surrounding it. The rich soils of the Thames Valley in particular attracted vast numbers of market gardens while large quantities of fruit were cultivated in Kent and vegetables were grown in Essex. Further out, vegetables, especially carrots were grown in profusion around Biggleswade in Bedfordshire. Biggleswade carrots arrived in London by the ton, courtesy of the Great Northern Railway. Ironically, the railways carried another kind of cargo out of London to the growers. This was the euphemistically-named nightsoil, the contents of closets, as well as scooped up horse-droppings. The horse was the prime mover of the London streets and hundreds of tons of dung were deposited on the streets every day. Both human and equine waste made excellent fertiliser.

If there can be said to have been a general pattern, it was that land used as market gardens close to central London often quickly disappeared under bricks and mortar and so new market gardens areas opened up on the periphery only to be gradually pushed further out as London expanded outwards. The railways had something to do with this

RAILWAY CRIME

Introduction

Railway stations from the start attracted all manner of human detritus. London's termini might almost have been designed with society's drifters in mind. In most cases they provided open access to covered space twenty-four hours a day. For the homeless that offered somewhere to get their head down which was better than dossing elsewhere under the stars.

London's major termini have also attracted a diverse seam of people operating just inside or definitely outside the law. Those offering freelance but illicit porterage services, for example; female prostitutes and rent boys; procurers and procuresses; touts of all sorts; robbers; cadgers; those bent on sexual assault eying up their potential victims – likewise those bent on robbery; cowboy horse-cab operators; conmen looking for gullible marks; rich men, poor men, beggarmen, thieves.

London has long attracted inward migration from the provinces. People came because they hoped or believed that London offered them a better future. The size of London, the wealth generated and displayed there, its anonymity and the opportunities it offered for criminal activity, have also attracted casual and career criminals, some of whom found rich pickings. London has also always drawn to it the vulnerable and the dysfunctional. They have included young people trying to get away from physical and other types of abuse at home; the bored and disaffected; drug addicts, even in the nineteenth century; those trying to escape from something but not necessarily knowing what it was; those hoping that a move to London might kick-start a new and better phase in their dreary lives. Many of these drifters were not well-equipped to deal with the dangers and temptations offered by the Metropolis. Many were lured into the sex trade. This hotchpotch of humanity has tended to arrive particularly at those London termini of services originating in the north of England and from Scotland. Many of them were scared, callow, vulnerable, in some cases literally children. A reception committee of low-life characters would be waiting to 'befriend' them as soon as they got off the train.

Pickpockets found rich rewards for their efforts in densely-crowded railway stations and carriages. In the latter, a common ploy was for a pickpocket with charm and plausibility to express concern for a wealthy-looking traveller and to offer to swap seats, away from a draught, for example. The thief would already have noted the disposition of likely valuables about the victim's person and in the minor melee created by changing seats in the crowded compartment, any useful items would be deftly removed. The skill required not only to remove the items without being detected but also in picking the right victim and obtaining agreement for the move while timing all this for just before a station stop at which the thief alighted, should not be underestimated. A journalist interviewed a retired thief who earned his crust by passing his skills on who declared with considerable pride that it was "as much a fine art as pianoforte-playing or high-class conjuring."

Another kind of villain was the luggage or baggage thief. One of the most spectacular hauls made by such operators occurred in the 1870s at Paddington Station. A member of the Countess of Dudley's entourage foolishly placed her employer's jewel-box on the floor for a few seconds while assisting a colleague. The box vanished in a trice. The contents which consisted of diamonds worth £50,000 were never recovered.

ASSAULTS AND ROBBERIES ON TRAINS

Many early passenger carriages contained a number of compartments which could be the scenario for any number of unpleasant experiences. Even first-class compartments brought travellers into close proximity with their fellows. A crowded carriage might enforce undesirably close physical intimacy but those of a nervous disposition might find this easier to handle than occupying a compartment with just one other passenger. The stranger might turn out to be a robber, a sexual predator with curious or repulsive preferences, a homicidal maniac, a chain-smoker or a mind-numbingly tedious bore. People felt trapped in these compartments and although of course the vast majority of journeys were completed without anything untoward happening, the fearful reality was that there was no ready way to stop the train or even to alert a member of the crew. Travellers therefore sometimes equipped themselves with weapons including firearms when they travelled by train. Women travellers often had a hat pin at the ready.

It was always felt that female travellers were particularly vulnerable to sexual and other forms of assault. For this reason some compartments were designated 'Ladies Only'. Of course simply labelling a compartment for the exclusive use of women travellers did not of itself prevent some determined male reprobate from jumping in when the guard's back was turned. The odds were then on that the blackguard would proceed to subject his female victim to a fate worse than death.

It was by no means unknown for prostitutes to ply their trade with punters in otherwise empty first-class compartments. The especially determined ones thought nothing of ejecting a single female occupant and replacing her with the client of the moment. Ideally the trains used for such activities were not all-stations stopping trains on busy suburban routes. However it was known that skilled prostitutes with able-bodied punters could complete the business in the five minutes it took a train to travel from London Bridge to Cannon Street Station.

It was not unknown for men travelling in a compartment with just one unknown woman to find themselves on the other end of the 'fate worse than death' situation. Women passengers sometimes maliciously concocted stories that a male fellow-passenger had made indecent comments or suggestions or had molested or sexually assaulted them. If there were no witnesses, the man, even if he was totally innocent, might find that his guilt was taken for-granted and he would go on to undertake a lengthy prison sentence. A woman who shared a compartment with a male passenger on a train from Watford Junction to Euston alleged that he had indecently assaulted her. The case went to court but was dismissed. She had unwisely informed the court that the dastardly fellow had smoked a pipe throughout the whole journey. The court considered that smoking a pipe and conducting a sexual assault were mutually exclusive activities. However it is no wonder that some men studiously avoided entering a compartment containing a lone female traveller just as some other men with evil intentions would have made a beeline for one.

Only members of the cloth seem to have been able to come through a compromising situation with their innocence generally being presumed. We shall never know exactly what was said or what went on when a young curate entered a compartment containing just a sixteen-year-old girl on a train of the Great Western Railway leaving Paddington. The girl alleged that he pulled her onto his knee, kissed her swan-like neck and whispered various over-familiar observations and suggestions into her ear. The case went to court, the curate denying all accusations of wrongdoing on his part. He did admit that he had entered into conversation with the girl and after some while had suggested that he might be able to get her a job playing the organ in his parish church. He also admitted having boasted that it was indeed a magnificent organ. Could this innocent comment have been misconstrued? The court thought that he had uttered it in good faith and the curate was able to return to his parish with his reputation unsullied.

In 1864 a gentleman was happily sitting in the compartment of a London & South Western Railway train out of Waterloo. He himself was travelling between Surbiton and Woking. He was startled out of his ruminations when he found himself staring into a woman's face a few inches from his but on the outside of the rapidly moving train. She was standing on the footboard of the carriage and clinging on for dear life. It was no easy matter to haul her to safety but fortunately some people by the side of the line had also seen her predicament and alerted the guard who brought the train to a swift halt. A dastardly character called Nash had earlier entered a compartment containing two women travellers, one of whom was of course the woman travelling in this unusual and extremely hazardous fashion. Her name was Mary Moody. The blackguard had attempted, without finesse, to chat the other woman up but she had alighted at Surbiton. When this happened, Mary decided to follow but her reactions were not quick enough and before she could gather up her things, the train began to pull away from the platform. She thus found herself alone with her singularly repulsive male fellow-traveller. Without further ado, he began to ask her a string of questions full of sexual innuendo. Mary's silence seemed only to have inflamed his passion because he first embraced her and then attempted an indecent assault. This was the cue for Mary to try to evade his clutches and escape by the daring and dangerous means of the compartment door and carriage footboard of the moving train. Readers will be relieved to know that Nash served time for this crime.

Assault was not always intentional. A man had been attacked by footpads near Willesden Junction Station. He had scared them off when he took out a pistol and fired over their heads. So elated was he by this robust defence of his person and property that a few days later he was relating the event to a stranger on a train. Warming to his theme, he got a trifle carried away and suddenly decided to show the stranger how he had dealt with the would-be robbers. He whipped out his pistol and fired it. His aim was not as true as it should have been because instead of the bullet passing over the traveller's head, it made a neat parting in his hair!

THE MURDER OF THOMAS BRIGGS ON THE NORTH LONDON RAILWAY

Britain in general and London in particular were shocked and horrified by what was claimed to be the first murder on a railway train. This happened at the perhaps surprisingly late date of 1864. Thomas Briggs was an aldermanic figure, the epitome of Victorian middle-class respectability. He was a widower 69 years of age, tall, silver-haired, dapper and distinguished-looking. He was also very fit for his age. He was the chief clerk of a banking house in the City. When travelling to and from work he wore a distinctive tall silk hat. He sported an expensive-looking gold chain stretched across his capacious midriff, the chain being attached to a fine gold watch. He carried a bag in one hand, a stout walking stick in the other.

On 9 July 1864 which was a Saturday, he left the office around half-past four to travel to Peckham for dinner with his niece of whom he was very fond. It was still light when he left to catch a horse bus back to King William Street in the City. He then walked briskly to Fenchurch Street Station where he entered a first-class compartment on a train of the North London Railway. He was alone when the train puffed out of Fenchurch Street at 9.50 pm to start on its roundabout route to his destination at Hackney via Shadwell, Stepney and Bow. Much of the route ran on low viaducts which gave a bird's eye view of the rooftops of inner-city working-class housing interspersed with the myriad of small, often noxious industrial premises then so characteristic of this part of London's East End. Hackney, however, where Briggs lived, was a cut above, boasting a respectable gentility.

The North London Railway had just over thirteen miles of its own line but its trains also ran on over fifty miles of line belonging to other companies. The NLR had an importance out of all proportion to its size because its small network linked the main lines coming into London from the north and west with the City and the docks in the east. The company's first terminus was a shared one at Fenchurch Street but it later opened a fine station of its own at Broad Street. It may have been a small company but it was a proud one and at this time it had little interest in the lower end of the travel market. Until 1875 it catered only for first and second class passengers. It possessed a fleet of small but powerful 4-4-0 tank engines and its four-wheeled carriages were quite luxurious by the standards of the time.

It was a warm evening and almost dark as the train trundled along. A weak light in the ceiling provided only partial illumination. Briggs had eaten well. He had worked all day. He dozed fitfully. At Bow he exchanged pleasantries through the open carriage window with an acquaintance called Lee who later averred there were two other passengers in the compartment. Lee remembered being mildly surprised to see Briggs travelling at such a late hour. He was also surprised by the appearance of the other two occupants of the carriage. They had not, in his opinion, looked like first-class travellers. Later, when being cross-examined in court, he admitted he had had a drink or two in a local pub.

The train pulled out of Bow, being due to arrive at the next stopping place, Victoria Park, Hackney Wick, in a few minutes. The next compartment to that occupied by Briggs was also first class and was occupied by a draper called Withall and a female traveller. They were not together. As the train was approaching Victoria Park, Withall described how he had heard a sudden and weird howling noise, reminiscent, he said, of a dog in distress. His unknown female companion made a remark to the same effect. In another compartment close by, a female passenger had the unpleasant experience of being spattered with drops of blood that came in through the open window. She said that she heard no untoward noises.

When the train arrived at Victoria Park, two young men-about-town, Henry Verney and Sydney Jones, made to join the train and they stepped into the compartment in which Briggs had started his journey. It was empty but although it was poorly-lit, they soon realised that a lot of blood was scattered around the compartment. A number of personal items could be made out. They included a black leather bag and a walking stick. Under the seat lay a black beaver hat, so squashed that it looked as if someone had stood on it. Thoroughly alarmed, they managed to get the attention of the guard who directed them to another compartment. It was obvious to the guard that the compartment had very recently witnessed foul play. He locked the compartment and gave instructions for a telegraph message to be sent to the superintendent at Chalk Farm, the station where the train terminated. There the carriage was uncoupled and shunted into a siding to await examination by the police.

Meanwhile the driver of a train proceeding in the opposite direction saw a dark object lying close to the track. He brought his train to a halt and he, the fireman and the guard descended to track level to investigate. They found that the object was the body of a man, battered and bloodied but still alive, although only just. A doctor was soon on the scene. His initial impression was that the injuries on the left hand side of the man's head had probably been sustained by his fall from a train. However, two violent blows had fractured his skull. Briggs, for it was he, died late the next evening. He never regained consciousness.

This horrible murder stirred up a hornet's nest of outraged headlines and scaremongering articles in the newspapers. 'Murder on the Iron Way' was true and comparatively moderate. Perhaps more typical was the newspaper which thundered, 'Who is safe?' If we may be murdered thus we may be slain in our pew at church, or assassinated at our dinner table'.

This first railway murder emphasised just how vulnerable passengers in compartments could be to the depredations of malefactors, even in the biggest city in the world. They dared not leap from the train while it was in motion. They had no way of stopping the train. It was not easy to attract the attention of the guard or the men on the footplate. Without a side-corridor in the carriage, it was difficult to gain the attention of travellers in other compartments. There was little that other travellers could do even if they had been alerted to possible trouble. Now two passengers travelling in the same compartment but who were strangers would spend the journey eyeing each other up suspiciously, making sure valuable possessions were out of sight. The manufacturers of coshes, then more generally known as life-preservers, had their workers slaving away on overtime in order to keep up with demand.

A massive murder enquiry was launched and came up with frustratingly few leads while the newspapers scarcely helped, clamouring as they do for a quick result. Clues pointed to a young German man called Franz Muller, living in digs in the East End. He was known to have boarded a ship in the London Docks, bound for New York and a new start in life. Two detectives set off for New York in a faster vessel and were waiting for Muller when he arrived there. He was searched and Briggs's gold watch was found as was the old man's hat to which Muller had made some modifications. He was extradited, brought back to England and his trial began at the Old Bailey began on 27 October. Muller looked small, even frail and certainly not the man to launch a murderous attack on Briggs who, despite being much older, was larger, stronger and fit for his age. It seemed likely that Muller had had an accomplice but who was he and why did Muller insist that he had been on his own? The case attracted enormous public interest and not a little xenophobia. The evidence was largely circumstantial but the jury took only fifteen minutes to reach their verdict. The execution was set for 8 a.m on in the morning of 14 November. The location was outside the hated Newgate Prison.

The crowds that gathered at hangings were known for being boisterous and badly behaved but the impending death of Muller seems to have attracted the most bestial and wretched of London's population, to a total of about 50,000, all baying for blood and avid for entertainment. The executioner was William Calcraft who, despite a long career in the terminatory business, was never much of a craftsman and he was unpopular not only with his victims, which was entirely understandable, but also with aficionados of a good hanging.

Franz Muller. Did he have an accomplice?

SHOWING WHAT A WONDERFUL IMPROVEMENT THE HOLES IN THE RAILWAY
CARRIAGES ARE, PARTICULARLY DURING THE HOLIDAYS.

A 'Muller Window'.

As *The Times* newspaper reported, the crowd went quiet only as Calcraft was doing his grisly work and Muller's life was ebbing away. Then there was an awed hush. For the rest of the time, there was 'loud laughing, oaths, fighting, obscene conduct and still more filthy language'. So horrible was the behaviour of the crowd at Muller's execution that the event undoubtedly contributed greatly to the developing feeling that executions should be made into private affairs carried out behind prison walls. Indeed, it was only about four years later that the last public hanging took place in Britain, again outside Newgate.

It has entered the annals of folklore that Muller was goaded into making a last-minute admission of guilt by the pastor attending him. Whether or not this is true, it is unlikely that any modern court would have passed such a verdict with the forensic and other investigative techniques now known.

As mentioned above, Muller had altered the hat he had stolen from Briggs into a kind of cut-down topper and these became fashionable among young-men-about-town in London. 'Muller Hats' enjoyed several years as fashion items.

On a positive note, some good can be said to have come of the murder of Thomas Briggs because methods of communication between passengers and what would now be called 'train crew' began slowly to come into use across the railway system. These went under the generic name of 'communication cord' and when activated they warned the engine driver to stop the train as soon as it was safe to do so but it was many years before such apparatus became mandatory. At least one observer commented that a communication cord would not have saved the life of Briggs. The first blow would probably have rendered him unable to summon assistance. The London & South Western Railway put small openings rather like portholes in the dividing partition between compartments and these at least offered some opportunity for frightened passengers to attract attention. Unfortunately these were often used by 'peeping toms' to observe the antics of courting couples in the adjacent compartment.

In the words of the counsel for the prosecution, "The crime…is almost unparalleled in this country. It is a crime which strikes at the lives of millions. It is a crime which affects the life of every man who travels upon the great iron ways of this country…a crime of a character to arouse in the human breast an almost instinctive spirit of vengeance." The first railway murder may have been a long time in coming but when it did, it chilled and horrified the entire nation.

AN UNSOLVED MURDER ON THE LONDON & SOUTH WESTERN RAILWAY

The public find murders fascinating. They find unsolved murders even more fascinating. One such murder took place on a suburban train of the L & SWR on its way from Hounslow to Waterloo. The year was 1897.

Elizabeth Camp was an attractive, intelligent working-class woman aged thirty-three. She was the manageress of a busy pub in the Walworth district of South London but this was her day off. She was having a very busy day. In the morning she went to Hammersmith to visit her younger sister and then travelled on to Hounslow for tea with her elder sister. Elizabeth was due shortly to get married and she had been shopping for various items connected with the forthcoming nuptials. She always enjoyed spending time with her sister of whom she was very fond. She was therefore feeling pleasantly content when she returned to Hounslow Station to catch the 7.42 to Waterloo. She had even managed to fit in a quick drink in a pub with her sister and a man euphemistically described as a 'friend of the family'. As if all this was not enough, her fiancé, Edward Barry, was due to meet her at Waterloo and they intended to visit a music-hall. Elizabeth was somewhat encumbered by the parcels and packages containing the articles she had bought as she selected an empty second-class compartment. Unfortunately, she was never to leave that compartment alive.

Edward was a good-looking, steady man but a bit of a worrier who tended to fuss and mother-hen his loved one. As was his way, he got to Waterloo in plenty of time to meet Elizabeth's train which was due to arrive at 8.23. He was most put out when the train arrived and he was unable to pick her out of the throng of passengers coming through the ticket barrier. It was most unlike her not to be where she said she was going to be.

Inevitably he soon got himself in a bit of a flap. Had she been on the train but somehow they had managed not to see each other? Was she at this moment wandering around the huge station looking for him? What time was the next train from Hounslow due? Edward fussed here and he fussed there, getting more agitated by the minute. He returned to the barrier and could not help noticing a knot of agitated-looking railway workers around an open compartment door of the train from Hounslow. Anxiety and a sense of foreboding welled up in Edward, not helped when two uniformed railway police officers made their way briskly to the carriage.

The practice at Waterloo was for cleaners to service the train before it left for another foray into London's south-western suburbia. Elizabeth's body had been discovered by a cleaner as he opened the compartment door. Her head and torso were largely under the seat and her legs were spread widely on the floor. A growing pool of blood was oozing from the corpse. With scant regard for possible evidence at the scene, the body was lifted out onto the platform. The dead woman had clearly been the victim of an exceptionally brutal attack in which she had been beaten to death and her skull had been stove in. There was blood everywhere and even to an unpractised eye, it was clear that the victim had not gone to her death without a ferocious fight back.

The body was removed to the mortuary at St Thomas's Hospital. With his heart in his mouth, Edward followed. When he got there, he made it clear who he was and he was called upon to identify the battered corpse. The worst-case scenario he could ever have anticipated lay in front of his horrified eyes.

The police scoured the compartment for clues. Apart from clearly having witnessed a struggle to the death, the only item that rendered any possible evidence was a bone cuff link on the floor. No trace of Elizabeth's train ticket was found but then the purse which she habitually carried could not be found either. If the motive was robbery, why had one or two jewellery items of minor value not been taken? Why should a would-be robber pick on a fit-looking youngish working-class woman who was well-dressed but clearly not affluent? Surely a better-off but weaker victim could have been found by the unknown assailant if he had only exercised some degree of patience?

The salaciously-minded quickly homed in on the idea that the motive of the attacker was sex. Cheap, sensational and melodramatic fiction of the Victorian period found a rich seam in the horrible fates that might fall innocent maidens at the hands of male malefactors travelling in enclosed railway compartments. Any male over the age of puberty was a potential sex-fiend stalking railway stations in order to locate and molest vulnerable women, happily subjecting them to a fate worse than death. However Elizabeth had not been sexually assaulted and the frequency of the station stops hardly allowed time for a successful assault on a woman as fit and strong as Elizabeth had been. However, a horribly violent murder had clearly taken place. What was the motive of the murderer? Who, indeed, was the murderer?

The police investigation quickly concluded that since Elizabeth's blood was still warm when her corpse was delivered to St Thomas's, she almost certainly had been killed towards the end of her journey from Hounslow and that her attacker had therefore probably left the train at one of the last three stops before Waterloo. These stations were not particularly busy at that time of the evening and it was hoped that questioning the staff who had been on duty might provide information about anyone seen with blood-stained clothing or acting in any way suspiciously. The resulting enquiries produced nothing. However, when the side of the line between Putney and Wandsworth was searched, a heavy porcelain pestle was found. It had blood and human hair adhering to it. The hair had belonged to Elizabeth Camp. The police now had the murder weapon. Appeals for anyone to come forward who recognised it drew a total blank. Next an appeal was issued for anyone who had been travelling on the 7.42 from Hounslow to come forward. This did not produce useful information either.

Gradually the furore over Elizabeth's murder died down as the papers found new horrors to gorge on. Police enquiries continued but were scaled down. It was revealed that Elizabeth had been engaged to a barman called Brown and that the relationship had ended very acrimoniously. Apparently Elizabeth had lent him money, some of which he had not repaid. Anonymous threatening letters had been sent to Elizabeth which the police thought had been written by Brown. Owing her money and apparently still smarting with resentment at the way he thought he had been treated, he had a motive for the murder but he also turned out to have a cast-iron alibi.

There is a lot of painstaking sweat and often little glory in routine police work. As enquiries continued, the police established that Elizabeth was something of a money-lender. Such people are generally disliked. Edward had told the police that Elizabeth frequently carried a considerable amount of money on her person. Could her murderer have been someone who knew this and had waited for an opportunity to rob her when she was alone? Many people owed her money. Could it have been one of her creditors? One of the creditors turned out to be the 'friend of the family' who had joined Elizabeth and her sister for a drink at Hounslow before she had left to return to Waterloo. His name was Stone. He had left Elizabeth and her sister before they went to the station to do some business elsewhere but since he knew which train Elizabeth was catching, the police wondered whether in fact he had entered the train unseen, alighted at an intermediate station and then, intent on murdering the woman to whom he owed money, joined Elizabeth in her compartment. He had the motive and the opportunity. However, the means were problematical. Was he in the habit of carrying a heavy pestle around with him? Or had he secreted it around his person because he knew that Elizabeth would be visiting Hounslow that day and returning to London on a little-used train?

Stone became the prime suspect and the police grilled him thoroughly. Reluctantly they had to let him go because, they said, there was insufficient evidence to obtain a conviction.

Although the newspapers hinted that the public were not being given the whole story, the case had now run out of steam and the murder of Elizabeth Camp on the 7.42 from Hounslow to Waterloo remains unsolved to this day.

An Appointment with the Hangman at Newgate

Louisa Masset lived in Stoke Newington, N16. She was half-French, half-English and thirty-three years of age when she hit the headlines in 1899. She lived with her married sister and her husband and was an unmarried mother with a small boy called Manfred. She had left France because of the stigma attached to the mothers of illegitimate children. She was a governess and teacher of piano. The child's natural father paid for Manfred to be cared for by a foster-mother in Tottenham. Louisa saw him regularly. She very much had a mind of her own and was no respecter of conventional mores and when a young Frenchman of nineteen called Eudor moved in next door, she was soon engaged in a steamy sexual relationship with him. The couple copulated as if there was no tomorrow and harboured no romantic notions about loving each other until the day they died.

Unexpectedly in October 1899, Manfred's father contacted Louisa requesting that he took on the job of looking after the boy. This seemed a good idea and she arranged to meet Manfred's foster-mother and pick the boy up. Before she did so, she put a brick into a bag which she then carried with her when she met him and took him to London Bridge Station. The date was 27 October. Later, a witness came forward to say that she had seen them together during the afternoon in the buffet at the station and that the little boy had seemed very distressed. The same witness saw Louisa again around six in the evening. She was alone. It transpired that she then went off with Eudor for a dirty weekend at Brighton.

It seems that between the first and second occasions she was seen at London Bridge, she had doubled back to north London. In the late afternoon, two women found the naked body of a small boy in the waiting room at Dalston Junction station on the North London Railway. It was immediately obvious to the police that he had been battered with a brick which was close by – in two pieces – and then suffocated. Press statements were issued and a murder hunt was launched.

On 30 October, Helen (the foster-mother) received a letter from Louisa telling her that Manfred was now in France and safe and sound but missing her awfully. By now all London was buzzing with speculation about the murdered infant. Helen was horribly suspicious that the description of the body matched that of Manfred and she went to the police. She provided an official identification. Meanwhile a bundle of little boy's clothes had been found at Brighton Station and Helen confirmed that they belonged to Manfred. Louisa was traced, arrested and charged with the murder. She stood trial at the Old Bailey and was found guilty. She was hanged at Newgate on 9 January 1900 after confessing to the murder but without providing a plausible reason for the horrible crime. Perhaps she did it because she lacked a strong maternal streak especially given her sexual obsession with Eudor. Louisa Masset was the first person to be hanged in Britain in the twentieth century.

CAUGHT BY THE TELEGRAPH

This was the case of a murderer who used the railway in an attempt to leave the scene of his dastardly crime and to evade detection. It was also the first case in which the electric telegraph, developed to help safety and communication on the railways, proved how effective it could be in apprehending a suspect on the run. Even those who had no interest in railways and little understanding of electricity would have pricked up their ears in 1845 when the telegraph played a vital role in the apprehension of a suspected murderer.

In 1839 William Fothergill-Cooke and Charles Wheatstone convinced the directors of the Great Western Railway to install a modified version of their electric telegraph system on the main line out of London as far as Hanwell. It was successful and in 1842 it was extended to Slough. All sorts of messages could now be transmitted quickly to assist the safe and efficient running of the line. Soon other companies were adopting the Cooke and Whetstone system and it was to become almost universal across Britain's burgeoning railway system.

John Tawell was a success – or so it seemed. He was intelligent, resourceful, persuasive and personable. His business interests were successful enough to provide him with a lifestyle of some luxury. He was also a devout member of his local Quaker community. However, Tawell had both a murky past and a murky present. When scarcely out of his teens, he had been sentenced to transportation for forgery. His conduct in the Australian penal colony had been exemplary and he had returned to England as a 'ticket-of-leave' man, essentially being licensed for good behaviour. He had learned from his experience. He did not fancy a return to the Antipodes but knew he was plausible and he fancied enriching himself without having to resort to indictable crime. He went down one of the well-worn paths of the con-man. He insinuated himself into the affections of a rich widow, a Quaker like himself and after they married, he gained access to her large bank account. He quickly discovered that he had a penchant for extra-marital affairs. His charm and preparedness to throw his money around made for rich pickings.

One of these affairs was with Sarah Hart who was a former servant of his. He set her up in a cottage in Slough discreetly out of the public eye but not so far that he couldn't slip down there for periodic sessions of rumpy-pumpy. He fathered a couple of children with Sarah for whom he accepted total financial responsibility. He always made sure that she had what he thought was enough money not only for all the basics but also for a more-than-comfortable life. Sarah, like other kept women, enjoyed spending her keeper's money but something was missing. This was the opportunity to socialise and move around freely. Ostracism in fact went with the way of life. However things began to change when Tawell retired from business which meant a significant fall in his income and in what he was prepared to give Sarah. Tensions now began to enter the relationship. She resented having less money to spend without anything to compensate her for her reduced circumstances. He, for his part, grew increasingly fed up with her constant complaints. As so often happens, their relationship quickly went from tranquil to tempestuous.

If Tawell had ever actually been in love with Sarah, he was now definitely out of love. She had become a burden and so he resolved to kill her. He made his preparations with some care. On 1 January 1845 he bought some prussic acid at a chemist's shop in the City of London and then cashed a cheque on one of his bank accounts although he knew he did not have the funds to support it. He called in at a City coffee house where he was known, to ascertain what time it closed in the evening. He then headed for Paddington and caught the 4 pm local train to Slough. He arrived at Sarah's cottage about 5 pm. It seems that the couple started off the evening in friendly enough fashion because Sarah made two visits to a nearby pub to buy some bottles of stout. Later the mood between the couple deteriorated because neighbours heard them arguing. Shouts turned to female screams of pain and Tawell was seen making his way from the cottage clearly in a great state of agitation. Another witness saw him heading for the station. A neighbour was trying to comfort Sarah and a doctor had been called for but she died just as he arrived. A local priest was called and he set off in his pony and trap for the station just as fast as he could go. It seemed likely that Tawell had caught a train back to Paddington. He persuaded the staff to telegraph to Paddington requesting that Tawell be arrested on arrival. The police were indeed waiting but instead of arresting him, they followed him to his lodgings.

Tawell was arrested the next day. He initially denied having been in Slough the previous evening or even of knowing anyone who lived there. In a rather patronising way he told them that his social status put him above suspicion. They must have enjoyed disabusing him of this notion when they charged him with murder.

The trial began on 12 March 1845 at Aylesbury and it excited enormous interest. The evidence suggested that Tawell had somehow managed to place some prussic acid in the stout that Sarah was drinking and that was the cause of death. On the third day, the jury retired to consider their verdict and returned quickly with the bald statement 'guilty'. Although this was not entirely unexpected, the verdict was met with ooh's and aah's and it seems that Tawell, as has been the case with other male murderers, had elicited the adoration of some of the women in the public gallery who wept openly and loudly when the sentence of death was pronounced on their hero.

On 28 March Tawell was hanged at Aylesbury. The case is famous less, perhaps, for the nature of the murder than for the fact that Tawell was the first murderer to be apprehended by the authorities using the high speed form of communication which had just become available courtesy of Cooke and Wheatstone's electric telegraph. Since the Great Western Railway played something of a pioneering role so far as the electric telegraph is concerned, it is worth musing on the idea that if Tawell had used another railway to make his way to and from his dastardly deed, he might have got away with it.

TERRORISM ON THE RAILWAYS

The Irish Question has been a running sore in British political life for centuries. It could be argued that the British ruling class historically considered Ireland to be little more than a colony to be controlled and exploited for the benefit of the 'mother country'. Issues around the development of its economy, the ownership of its land and the toxic fall-out resulting from the clash of religious persuasions ensured that Ireland was at the forefront of the political agenda for much of the nineteenth century. Irish MPs sat in Westminster at a time when Irish nationalism was growing inexorably. By the

THE OLDEST *ACCIDENT OFFICE* IN THE WORLD

RAILWAY PASSENGERS ASSURANCE COMPANY

HEAD OFFICE 64, CORNHILL, LONDON, E.C.

The Shares of which are vested in & the Contracts of which are guaranteed by the
NORTH BRITISH & MERCANTILE INSURANCE CO.

INSURANCE AGAINST

ACCIDENTS

OF ALL KINDS

Accidents and Illness
Workmen's Compensation
Third Party Liability
Motor Car Risks
Burglary
Glass Breakage
Loss of Baggage
Live Stock

TICKETS insuring against Railway Accidents may be obtained at all Booking Offices of the L. & N.W. Railway—————— or direct from the *Head·Office at . . . . 64, CORNHILL, E.C.*

Boiler explosions, derailments and collisions were by no means uncommon until improved safety measures became widespread. Insurance could be bought by the passenger who was prepared for such an outcome of his journey.

1870s Home Rule was coming to dominate British politics. Irish nationalists became increasingly militant and vociferous and their frustration meant that some, inevitably, turned away from the ballot box and towards the bomb.

A serious phase of terrorist activity broke out in 1883. In London the first evidence of this was a large explosion outside government offices in March of that year. Police investigations revealed a terrorist cell based in the prestigious Charing Cross Hotel belonging to the South Eastern Railway. On the evening of 30 October two bombs went off on the underground within a few minutes of each other, fortunately without loss of life. The first was on a train near Praed Street (later Paddington) and it showered passengers with broken window glass. Five people needed hospital treatment. Shortly afterwards, a bomb exploded on a train between Charing Cross and Westminster. The lights went out and large amounts of black smoke gave the impression that the incident was more serious than it actually was. There were no major casualties.

In January 1884 information was received that one or more bombs were going to be detonated at St Pancras. For several days the Midland main line as far north as Leicester was subjected to large-scale close security but nothing untoward occurred. If disruption and diversion of resources had been intended, they were achieved. A couple of weeks later, five containers of explosives were found in Primrose Hill Tunnel on the LNWR line out of Euston. They lacked fuses and detonators and it was unclear how they got there and for what purpose.

A large explosion at the LBSCR side of Victoria on 26 February 1884 caused much damage and was followed by a fire, but with few casualties. Searches were made at other stations, bombs being found at Charing Cross and Paddington and, a week later, at Ludgate Hill Station. These devices offered the police a number of clues. Those responsible were Irish-Americans and some were arrested and convicted.

A lull in terrorist activity followed until 2 January 1885 when a bomb exploded on the Metropolitan Railway near Gower Street (later Euston Square Station). It was a device by the side of the line and it detonated at 9.14 when an Aldgate to Hammersmith train was passing. There was a loud and frightening explosion, the lights went out but casualties were again, thankfully, few. Police investigations led to the arrest, conviction and imprisonment of two men thought to be the ringleaders of the bomb cell. They received life sentences and with their enforced retirement, the bombing campaign ceased.

THE EARLY DAYS OF
RAILWAY BOOKSTALLS

From the earliest days of railways there seems to have been a largely unspoken assumption that travelling by train is intrinsically boring and that something was needed to relieve the tedium of the journey. Nature abhors a vacuum and so the railway bookstall made its appearance but not before vendors had been making their way up and down the platforms of the Liverpool and Manchester Railway's terminus stations selling newspapers and railway guides. This practice had certainly begun by 1839.

Soon it was found that a permanent fixture enabled a wider range of goods to be displayed and made available for sale. The bookstall was about to arrive, being the successor to the mobile vendor and his descendent the vendor with a simple little folding table displaying his wares. Some early bookstalls were staffed by former railway employees who had suffered injury in their employment and had to leave the service. On other occasions widows of former employees who had been fatally injured while on duty ran such stalls.

The railway companies concerned laudably displayed some social conscience while receiving the rents payable for the bookstalls and it wasn't long before entrepreneurs began to find that station bookstalls could be a profitable venture. The first in London and probably the first such enterprise in the UK was the bookstall set up by one William Marshall at Fenchurch Street Station in 1841. This stall represented a diversification for Marshall who already supplied newspapers wholesale to the Great Western Railway.

Alas for innocence! An indignant article appeared in *The Times* on 9 August 1851 in which the writer holds forth in disgust about bookstalls in general and those at the major London termini in particular. He had no problem with the sale of newspapers on these stalls but was not amused to find what he disparagingly referred to as 'French novels' hobnobbing on the shelves with beer bottles and various kinds of sweetmeat. Clearly the proprietors were pandering to the basest of tastes, so the writer fulminated. This article in fact was fairly moderate in tone compared with other contemporary accounts which described bookstalls as little better than brothels, attracting as they did such human detritus as pickpockets, prostitutes and drifters of all kinds. Those who owned the stalls were disreputable creatures only too happy to cater to their clients' basest instincts.

Clearly such observers enjoyed venting their self-righteous spleens after continually hanging around these bookstalls and noticing the comings and goings with evident prurient relish. It was ever thus with the chattering classes but enough of a fuss was made for a Parliamentary Select Committee to consider ways of monitoring and controlling the reading material sold on railway bookstalls.

Henry Walton Smith was a wholesale newsagent busily and lucratively engaged in distributing London newspapers and other periodicals by rail to provincial towns and cities. Bookstalls were getting a bad name and Smith saw an opportunity to clean up their tarnished image by providing railway travellers with more wholesome material in bookstalls of his own. In 1848 he successfully tendered for the exclusive right to provide stalls selling newspapers and periodicals on the stations of the LNWR in return for a yearly rent of £1500. Thus was born the 'W. H. Smith & Son' empire of reputable bookstalls. A refinement quickly added was the provision of small circulating libraries in his bookstalls. Even our self-righteous *Times* correspondent did his best to find what he called 'trash' on the W. H. Smith bookstall on Euston Station but failed in this worthy task. By this time Smith's rather prudish expurgation of the literature his stalls sold had earned him the nickname 'Old Morality'. Soon Henry Walton Smith's bookstalls were providing a service to the public on railways as diverse as the London & South Western, the Lancashire & Yorkshire and the North British. In 1863 Smith bought out the smaller chain of bookstalls owned by Horace Marshall, son of the pioneering William Marshall. Rumblings about the vacuity, if no longer about the salaciousness at worst or the sheer lack of literary merit of the literature sold on station bookstalls, continued for many years. In 1855 the novelist Anthony Trollope who travelled extensively on the railway, described the novels he found on station bookstalls as the very worst of their kind. Several publishers produced cheap, often paper-covered editions of their titles for sale in the bookstall trade. Routledge, for example, had a series called 'Railway Library'. When this venture ended after fifty years, it had produced no fewer than 1,300 titles. It is likely that railway bookstalls overall were one of a number of agencies in the Victorian period which brought literature to an increasingly wide audience. The W. H. Smith bookstalls, for example, sold vast numbers of cheap editions of the 'Waverley' novels written by Sir Walter Scott.

W. H. Smith did not have things all his way in Scotland and found a doughty opponent in John Menzies & Co who completely saw him off north of the Border but his stalls soon came to provide a useful service not only on the concourses of the mighty London termini but on hundreds of main line, branch and underground stations in London and its hinterland. His domination of bookstall provision at these stations did not go unchallenged particularly after 1900 but he remained pre-eminent in the business.

LINES TO THE
CRYSTAL PALACE

Londoners and others did not want 'their' Crystal Palace in Hyde Park to be dismantled once the Great Exhibition was over. Few buildings seem to have elicited so much affection so quickly. However the terms under which it had been erected in a Royal Park required its swift removal. It was carefully dismantled – its prefabricated structure being helpful in this respect — and stored. Sir Joseph Paxton created the Crystal Palace Company and then set about raising the finance to buy the building and re-erect it on a new site. The chosen site was 200 acres of parkland with many mature trees at Sydenham Hill. It was a quiet rural spot with commanding views over London. The idea was to build what would probably nowadays be described as a multiplex leisure 'experience' at this point. At that time, reflecting different values, it was designed to be a centre of recreation, culture and education.

The new Crystal Palace building was considerably larger and grander than its predecessor which had stood in Hyde Park. Huge amounts of money were spent to furnish the interior with items chosen to depict the art and architecture of the great civilisations of the past. Exotic plants were obtained for the grounds and also a superb collection of palms which had to be kept in tropical conditions within the main building. There were many permanent exhibits concerned with natural history and anthropology. The gardens were to be on a grand scale comparable with the best in Europe. Shows and exhibitions were to be laid on in the grounds and in the galleries of the huge building. The whole undertaking cost over £1.3 million to get it started. Two tall water towers at either end of the building provided the supply for the innumerable fountains and the humidity necessary in the parts of the building full of palms and other tropical exotica. These were designed by none other than I. K. Brunel and were just about the only items still standing after the disastrous fire that destroyed the building in 1936.

In the grounds a large number of life-size models of prehistoric creatures proved to be a never-ending source of fascination. They are still there and are one of the most tangible pieces of remaining evidence of this remarkable venture. The new Crystal Palace opened in an atmosphere of almost unalloyed celebration on 10 June 1854.

High hopes were entertained that the Crystal Palace with its permanent exhibits, its changing exhibitions and its galaxy of attractions to cater for all tastes would prove to be a venue drawing in people not only from Greater London but also from much of the south-east of England and even elsewhere. From the start it had been envisaged that railways would provide the means of mass transport for the crowds that would be needed if the venture was to be a financial success. Paxton had worked very closely with the London, Brighton & South Coast Railway. The Crystal Palace was close to stations at Sydenham and Penge on the LBSCR's route from London Bridge to Brighton but it was decided to maximise access to the new attraction by building a spur line from this route to a new station sited close to the Palace from which passengers would be able to walk under cover straight to the building. Passenger services began running into the Crystal Palace Station (later Crystal Palace Low Level) on the day the building was officially opened. The LBSCR directors were not disappointed by the Crystal Palace's ability to pull crowds. On one day in 1859, trains conveyed 112,000 people to the Palace of whom 70,000 had travelled via the line out of London Bridge. Another line, the West End of London & Crystal Palace Railway, not at first operated by the LBSCR but having good relationships with it, approached Crystal Palace from London via Balham, Streatham and Gypsy Hill. It was soon extended south and east to Norwood Junction and New Bromley (now Shortlands).

To serve the Palace and shift the crowds, the LBSCR built a very substantial station with a covered way of iron and glass up to the south end of the building. A siding was provided for the Crystal Palace Company and over the years many very strange items were loaded and unloaded at this point. Discounted tickets for travel and entry were available and through tickets were issued by other companies including the LNWR which enjoyed running powers to the LBSCR's Crystal Palace Station.

The London, Chatham & Dover Railway quickly decided that it wanted a serious slice of the action at the Crystal Palace and via a client company, the Crystal Palace & South London Junction Railway, completed a branch line in August 1865 from the Peckham Rye area through Honor Oak and Upper Sydenham to what eventually became known as the High Level station at Crystal Palace. Through trains from Victoria had

Crystal Palace High Level Station of the London, Chatham & Dover Railway. This imposing station gives some idea of the expectation for levels of passenger traffic. The tall thin buildings were water towers designed by I. K. Brunel. It was somehow typical of his works that when the Crystal Palace was destroyed by fire in 1936, almost the only structures left standing were Brunel's two towers.

to clamber up gradients as steep as 1 in 60 to reach the terminus. Just before reaching Crystal Palace the line passed through Paxton's Tunnel which was close to a fine house in which Paxton lived for several years. The last few miles of the line passed through a hilly, wooded district peppered with the villas of the affluent and which was never likely to have offered much originating traffic in the early days or indeed even up to the time of its closure in 1954 when of course recreational traffic to the Crystal Palace had long since ended.

The LCDR built a station at the end of the line which was so splendid that it immediately consigned even the very well-appointed Low Level Station to a definite second place. It had a trainshed of glass, iron and brick which cost over £100,000 neatly complementing the Palace itself and the whole place was expansive enough to have served as a terminus station in a major provincial city. Generous amenities were provided for passengers and those with first-class tickets even had their own access to the Palace. The whole building was designed to be able to handle vast crowds, up to 7,000 or 8,000 an hour and to do so in great style.

Clearly both the LBSCR and the LCDR invested a great deal of money in these lines and stations but did they provide the hoped-for financial rewards? Londoners were extremely proud and fond of their re-sited Crystal Palace but that doesn't necessarily mean that they flocked to it in great numbers, or at least in the numbers hoped for. In 1866 a fire destroyed the north transept and it was indicative of the Company's already rather forlorn hopes that it was never rebuilt. The Sabbatarian movement kept up the pressure to stop Sunday opening which meant that the Palace was largely prevented from opening precisely on the day when it could have expected the best crowds of the week. The Crystal Palace became famous for its magnificent fireworks displays staged by Messrs Brock & Co but many who watched them did so from afar and without paying to enter the grounds. By the 1890s, the glitter was definitely off the Crystal Palace and the Company was becoming increasingly insolvent. In 1913 a public subscription had to be raised in order to save the Crystal Palace. It and its two accompanying stations proved to be a white elephant. This was ironic because the Great Exhibition which had of course spawned the Crystal Palace had demonstrated so forcibly to the world how the railways could provide the means whereby vast numbers of people could travel easily and cheaply to enjoy a spectacle which so broadened their horizons.

We cannot leave the Crystal Palace without mentioning another fabled railway which ran in its grounds. In 1864 an experimental 'pneumatic' railway was built. It was effectively a development of Isambard Kingdom Brunel's unsuccessful atmospheric railway in south Devon. Brunel himself had been dead for five years. A passenger carriage ran on a broad gauge track for a distance of 600 yards through a tunnel, quickly and silently, linking the High and Low Level stations and the Palace itself. A return fare of 6*d*, expensive at the time, proved no deterrent to those who wanted to sample this novel form of propulsion. A single carriage running on broad gauge rails took passengers on the journey of less than a minute. The success of this small-scale operation encouraged proposals for what would have been London's first tube railway. It would have run from Whitehall to Waterloo under the Thames and work began but was abandoned in the financial crisis of 1866. It is said that the stub of this tunnel is still in place.

Fashion is capricious and in time the 'pneumatic railway' was closed down but before long a myth developed that the carriage remained within the bricked-up tunnel and

The pneumatic railway at Crystal Palace.

contained a grisly cargo of long-forgotten skeletal passengers. Traces of this tunnel could be seen for many years and in the early 1990s an edition of the *New Civil Engineer* carried an article with photographs taken many years earlier inside the tunnel. No abandoned carriage containing equally abandoned skeletons was to be seen. According to the article, no trace of the tunnel now survives.

SHERLOCK HOLMES AND LONDON'S RAILWAYS

Arthur Conan Doyle, the creator of the immortal Sherlock Holmes stories, was of solidly Victorian antecedents, having been born in Edinburgh to middle-class parents in 1859. He studied medicine at the local university where he met and was strongly influenced by one of his tutors, Dr Joseph Bell. He was greatly impressed by Bell's ability at intuitive but systematic deduction, a skill he sometimes used to amuse his students, perhaps scrutinising a latecomer to one of his lectures. Purely from visible clues and items about the student's person, he was able to construct an accurate resume of exactly where the tardy student had been in the last few hours and what he had been doing.

Doyle started writing embryonic stories when, as a doctor, he whiled away a few odd minutes waiting for his next patient. He showed them to friends who encouraged him to refine them and attempt to get them published. In Sherlock Holmes he created an apparently emotionless and ascetic private detective who used the kind of skills possessed by Bell and added to them a modern scientific and systematic study of evidence, particularly at the scene of the crime. He nearly always got his man with his relentless pursuit of the truth and yet, for all that, Holmes was a flawed hero. He had troughs of lethargy and despair during which he took narcotics. He could be untidy, rude and impatient of others who did not think as quickly as he did and he was given to playing the violin, often at unwonted times. Conan Doyle's masterstroke was to team him up with the brave, faithful and dogged Dr John Watson who constituted the perfect foil to the mercurial Holmes. He was the ordinary fellow with whom the reader could identify.

The first stories containing adventures involving Holmes were two novels which appeared in 1887 and 1890 which enjoyed considerable success and enabled the publishers of *The Strand* magazine to persuade the author to embark, probably not without some reluctance, on a series of serialised short stories which became extraordinarily popular. The short stories were brought together in book form, most of which appeared between 1891 and 1904. A longer story, the exceptionally spooky *The Hound of the Baskervilles*, was completed in 1902 and another novel, *The Valley of Fear*, was completed in 1915. Some other stories appeared later, well out of our timeframe, but experts (and there are many) consider that the general quality of the stories deteriorates over time and that in fact Holmes probably should never have come back after his apparently fatal plummet into the Reichenbach Falls while in the deadly embrace of his arch-enemy, the egregious Professor Moriarty. It is, of course, a matter of opinion.

Be that as it may, at their best the Sherlock Holmes stories are exceptionally evocative of the entrancing yet sinister gas-lit and foggy Metropolis of the late Victorian times in which they are mostly set and of the louche characters of its underworld who, almost always, come off second best when they pit their wits against Holmes, the master sleuth.

His investigations take him around London but also out of the Metropolis and he makes considerable use of its railways. It is hard to escape the impression that Conan Doyle was something of an enthusiast for railways and railway travel. He seemed to have his favourite stations and lines. Perhaps he liked the West Country because Paddington (for the GWR) and Waterloo (London & South Western Railway) feature more frequently than other termini and his stories loftily eschew any journeys from St Pancras (Midland Railway) even when a trip to the hills of Derbyshire is being undertaken. This is odd because he often tells Watson to 'look it up in Bradshaw', this being an authoritative monthly containing the timetables of the vast majority of Britain's railway companies, even if an IQ of formidable level was needed in order to extract the required information. Some of the routes used for journeys made by Holmes look at first sight to have either been impossible, difficult or inconvenient. On closer examination, however, it appears that Conan Doyle probably knew his 'Bradshaw' well and that leaving, say Victoria, for a journey into Surrey and then returning to Waterloo was actually perfectly feasible, if not necessarily the best or most obvious route. Not all Holmes' peregrinations make any kind of sense. Why, for example, should he and Watson join a train of the London, Chatham & Dover Railway at Victoria when their immediate destination is Newhaven on the LBSCR? They alighted at Canterbury and would have faced several changes in order to reach Newhaven. Or was it all a decoy to avoid the clutches of Professor Moriarty, Holmes' nemesis? Other London termini that Holmes used are London Bridge, Charing Cross, Liverpool Street and King's Cross. In *The Adventure of the Abbey Grange* Holmes and Watson take a cab through 'the opalescent London reek' to Charing Cross where they have tea in the refreshment room before joining their train.

Holmes excels himself in the adventure of *The Norwood Builder*. He and Watson are sitting in their chambers in Baker Street one morning bemoaning the lack of the kind of piquant cases on which they had been able to exercise their talents in the past. Suddenly a frantic-looking young man bursts into their room and announces, "I am the unhappy John Hector McFarlane." If he thought that his name would evoke instant recognition, McFarlane was disappointed. Holmes looked him up and down and then said, "You mentioned your name as if I should recognise it, but I assure you that, beyond obvious facts that you are a bachelor, a solicitor, a Freemason, and an asthmatic, I know nothing whatever about you." McFarlane is accused of murder over a will and he enlists Holmes' support in order to prove his innocence. Holmes quickly brings his rapier-like intellect to bear on the problem. He examines the will and then pronounces that, "It was written in a train: the good writing represents stations, the bad writing movement, and the very bad writing passing over points. A scientific expert would pronounce at once that this was drawn up on a suburban line, since nowhere save in the immediate vicinity of a great city could there be so quick a succession of points. Granting that his whole journey was occupied in drawing up the will, then the train was an express, only stopping once between Norwood and London Bridge." Holmes was right, of course, and he went on to demonstrate McFarlane's innocence.

The Bruce-Partington Plans was written in 1908 but set on a day of dense London fog in November 1895. The body of a young man, a government employee at Woolwich Arsenal, is found by the side of the Metropolitan Line close to Aldgate. He did not appear to have been robbed and in his pocket were papers giving details of a highly secret naval submarine. How had the young man whose name was Cadogan West come to be found dead by the railway and what was someone so junior doing with such sensitive items on his person, items that he would not have had official access to? The Metropolitan Railway was built on the 'cut-and-cover' principle and the location where the body was found was in the open air and on a curve just after the junction where a branch diverged for Aldgate East and Whitechapel. Holmes deduces that the body was placed on the top of a carriage of an Inner Circle Line train where it was open to the elements and regularly stopped for signals. He found such a location near Gloucester Road Station. Cadogan West's body then fell off its precarious perch as the train jerked over the junction points at Aldgate. The rest of the case was simplicity itself.

Holmes studiously avoided travelling on the Underground while moving around London, preferring horse-drawn cabs. These may have given more of a sense of place, something he clearly revelled in, and have been more convenient for door-to-door journeys but where they paralleled the lines of the growing underground railway network, they are likely to have been considerably slower. Sometimes speed was of the essence when he was on his missions. Was there a reason for Holmes' aversion to travelling on the Underground?

LONDON'S VICTORIAN RAILWAYS IN ART

Although London, because of the size and relative affluence of its population, had always been a significant manufacturing centre, the establishment of Britain's staple heavy industries, dependent on coal and steam power, was largely around the coal-producing districts elsewhere. Most of Britain's early railways were also to be found around those districts – after all, they were created primarily for the transport of coal and other bulky and heavy minerals.

Publishers offered commercial prints of varying quality of such major early lines as the Stockton & Darlington opened in 1825 and the Liverpool & Manchester in 1830. London's early railway development lagged behind. However the building of the first main line railway into London was recorded visually with a degree of detailed accuracy that had never been done before and has rarely been achieved since. It was the work of John Cooke Bourne (1814-96), an artist and lithographer. In 1836 he took to watching work progressing on the building of the London & Birmingham Railway into and out of Euston. He became so fascinated by the operations that he decided to produce a careful visual record of this civil engineering prodigy. Bourne was an extremely competent draughtsman with a superb understanding of line and form. He made many sketches of the work in the London area, including the construction of the Euston Arch and the Arch as completed and having won a powerful patron, he went on to have folios of tinted lithographs published of the continuing work through Camden and eventually all the way to Birmingham. Bourne's work is realistic and meticulous and provides vital historical evidence of the methods employed in the construction of this pioneering line. It also did a useful public relations job for the new-fangled railways whose disruption of and intrusion into both town and country was provoking considerable hostility at the time.

J. M. W. Turner (1775-1851) was one of Britain's most prolific and successful painters. His *Rain, Steam and Speed* of 1844 is included here because at least the train he shows was heading for Paddington and it is a classic. Turner provides an impression of a broad gauge steam-hauled train hurrying through a storm and passing over a bridge. It is actually the very shallow-arched bridge over the Thames just east of Maidenhead and Turner took several trips on trains to get the details for his composition. He stuck his head out of the window, sketching away, getting soaked in the process and almost certainly annoying his fellow-passengers who may not have appreciated the artistic genius at work in their midst. A boat drifts aimlessly on the river and a road bridge can be seen veering off to the left as if its purpose is being superseded by the new high-speed form of communication. Turner was fascinated by the harnessing of steam as a means of power and the painting shows a perhaps grudging admiration for the exciting new spectacle of a steam train at speed.

A somewhat neglected aspect of the art of the Victorian period is genre or figurative painting which depicts episodes from everyday life. From the point of view of social and cultural history, these works can be a source of valuable evidence. Some of them deal with scenes on railway stations and two of the best-known ones depict King's Cross and Paddington. *Going North, King's Cross Station* was produced in 1893 by George Earl (1824-1908). It depicts a crowded scene on the platform at King's Cross with a large party getting ready to join a train going up the East Coast Main Line to Scotland. It is August and the smart and clearly well-heeled travellers are gathering to go northwards for the grouse- shooting season. Their luggage, their weapons of mass destruction and their dogs are shown in realistic detail. This painting is one of a pair. The other is titled *Coming South, Perth Station* and it is September and the party are about to board the train back to London. Various stags' antlers, animal furs and hampers probably containing salmon are testimony to the party's successful depredations on the wild life of Scotland. It was a wonder there was any left if this haul was anything to go by.

W. P. Frith (1819-1909) specialised in genre paintings of crowd scenes. *The Railway Station* of 1862 is perhaps the best-known of all railway paintings and it contains an almost overwhelming amount of detail. It shows a departure platform at Paddington with passengers, luggage, servants and all, preparing for their journey. A small group of poor people can be seen on the left, hurrying in their anxiety to catch the train. In the centre Frith depicts some typical middle class people, including his own family and a bridal party. Their relative wealth means that they are used to trains and they are calm and unhurried. Towards the right of the picture two real-life detectives are arresting a well-dressed man almost certainly a white-collar criminal, before he can escape on the train. There is a comprehensive medley of other characters including a foreigner engaged in a dispute with a cabbie about his fare, a lady making a fuss about her baggage, a calm-looking station superintendent bent on making order out of chaos and a sportsman clearly departing on a fishing trip. In all Frith depicts eighty-six people including himself. The public loved the painting. The critics were less effusive. Despite all the action taking place in *The Railway Station*, Frith's painting is somewhat stuffy and it provoked some lesser artists into producing parodies of it.

James Tissot (1836-1902) was a French painter who fled Paris after the fall of the Commune in 1871 and stayed in Britain until 1882. He produced many paintings of fashionable society but also found inspiration for depictions of the Thames and other scenes around London. *Waiting for the Train* shows a well-dressed and clearly well-to-do young woman standing on a platform surrounded by her baggage awaiting the arrival of her train. The location is totally unrecognisable. She is standing on the main line platforms at a rural-looking Willesden Junction. Another delightful work by Tissot is titled *The Arrival Platform at Victoria Station*. Camille Pisarro (1830-1903) was a French Impressionist painter who spent some time in Britain and painted *The Station* in 1871. It depicts a train of the London, Brighton & South Coast Railway leaving Lordship Lane Station on the unsuccessful line to Crystal Palace High Level.

Waiting for the Train by James Tissot (1836-1902). The location of this charming painting is, almost unbelievably, the main line platforms at Willesden Junction!

Arrival Victoria also by Tissot.

Alarmed passengers look out of a train that has come to a sudden and unexpected halt. A passenger asks the guard what has happened. He replies that there is nothing to worry about — they have simply hit an excursion train. The jeremiahs of the day averred that travelling on excursion trains was inherently more dangerous than normal scheduled trains.

John O'Connor (1830-89) was an Irish painter who met with some success in London and left us with one particularly memorable painting, *St Pancras Hotel and Station from Pentonville Road*. The foreground is a lively depiction of the workaday Pentonville Road descending the side of the valley of the River Fleet. It is the sunset on what has been a fine day. Dominating the scene is the misty, almost ethereal outline of Scott's Midland Grand Hotel fronting Barlow's magnificent train shed. The domination by the hotel of its surroundings is absolute and yet there is also a sense of it being a vast mock-Gothic folly.

The impact of the railways on their viaducts over the working class districts through which they passed is brilliantly conveyed in one of the drawings in Gustav Dore's famous collection 'London: a Pilgrimage', published in 1872 and produced in conjunction with Blanchard Jerrold. It is titled *Over London – By Rail*. In the distance a steam train crosses a tall viaduct while belching out copious amounts of smoke and, doubtless, soot. Huddled in the shadow of the viaduct are monotonous rows of mean proletarian dwellings whose backyards are teeming with a cowed yet somehow dignified humanity. A sullen light hangs over the crowded scene – all is grey and grimy. It is realistic stuff — the depiction of the hard under-belly of nineteenth century capitalism and industrial exploitation (see p.8). Dore's London was a place on which the sun never shone. Dore (1832-83) was primarily a book illustrator and he produced a number of scenes on the London underground railways of the time which were realistic rather than heroic.

George Cruikshank (1792-1878) was a complex character perhaps best-known for his caricature work in which he was clearly influenced by earlier great exponents of the art such as Gillray. His work frequently has a moral purpose especially when he is attacking 'The Demon Drink'. He seems to have had little sympathy for the railways as demonstrated in the striking drawing in which the railway is portrayed as a demonic fire-breathing monster bearing down on a helpless family living in its path and who are just about to be either crushed to pieces by it or sucked up into its rapacious maw.

Punch; or the London Charivari, first appeared in July 1841. In its earliest days it was an unashamedly radical champion of the oppressed and a scourge of the established body politic. However, its satirical content proved successful with the Victorian middle classes, confident enough as they were of their position in the world's leading nation to be able to appreciate jokes against themselves. Who paid the piper called the tune and *Punch* evolved into an upholder of that complex set of notions that can be described as 'Victorian Values'. Be that as it may, those who wrote for and produced the illustrations for *Punch* found in railways an enormously rich seam of material perhaps mostly around the human quirks and foibles that railways and railway travel brought out. In its early days it inveighed against what it considered to be the arrogance and greed of railway companies, their directors and shareholders. Another periodical in which artwork depicting railways in London and elsewhere appeared was *The Illustrated London News*. It first appeared in 1842. The *ILN* had no satirical or humorous element, being more in the nature of a weekly newspaper but it contained many well-drawn pictorial images which provide valuable evidence of the impact of railways in London and elsewhere.

BIBLIOGRAPHY

Barker, F. & Hyde, R. *London as it might have been*, London, 1982

Barker, T. C. & Robbins, M. *A History of London Transport, Vol. 1*, London, 1975

Betjeman, J. & Gay, J. *London's Historic Railway Stations*, London, 1972

Biddle, G. *Victorian Stations, Railway Stations of England & Wales 1830-1923*, Newton Abbot, 1973

Binney, M. & Pearce, D. *Railway Architecture*, London, 1979

Brandon, D. & Brooke, A. *Blood on the Tracks, A History of Railway Crime*, Stroud, 2010

Brindle, S. *Paddington Station. Its History & Architecture*, Swindon, 2004

Brown, J. *London Railway Atlas*, first edition, Horsham (Surrey), 2006.

Carter, E. *A Historical Geography of the Railways of the British Isles*, London, 1959

Clayton, A. *Subterranean City, Beneath the Streets of London*, London, 2000

Course, E. *London's Railways*, London, 1962

Croome, D. F. & Jackson, A. A. *Rails through the Clay*, second edition, London, 1990

De Mare, E. *The London Doré Saw*, London, 1973

Douglas, H. *The Underground Story*, London, 1963

Dyos, H. J. & Wolff, M. *The Victorian City. Images and Realities, Vol II*, London, 1973

Ellis, C. Hamilton, *Railway Art*, London, 1977

Evans, A. H. B. & Gough, J. V. (Eds), *The Impact of the Railway on Society in Britain*, Aldershot, 2000

Freeman, M. *Railways in the Victorian Imagination*, New Haven & London, 1999

Gray, A. *Crime on the Line*, Penryn (Cornwall), 2000

Halliday, S. *Making the Metropolis. 1815-1914, Creators of Victoria's London*, Derby, 2003

Halliday, S. *Underground to Everywhere, London Underground's Railway in the History of The Capital*, Stroud, 2001

Jackson, A. A. *London's Local Railways,* second edition, London, 1999
Jackson, A. A. *London's Termini,* second edition, London, 1985

Kellett, J. R. *Railways & Victorian Cities,* London, 1969
Klapper, C. *London's Lost Railways,* London, 1976

Olsen, D. J. *The Growth of Victorian London,* London, 1976

Piper, D. *Artists' London,* London, 1982
Porter, R. *London. A Social History,* first edition, London, 1994

Richards, J. & McKenzie, J. *The Railway Station. A Social History,* Oxford, 1986

Sheppard, F. *The History of London. London 1808-1870: The Infernal Wen,* London, 1971
Sidney, S. *Rides on Railways, (Ed B.Trinder),* Chichester, 1973
Simmons, J. *St Pancras Station,* London, 1968
Simmons, J. *The Railway in Town & Country 1830-1914,* Newton Abbot, 1986
Simmons, J. *The Victorian Railway,* London, 1991
Smith, G.R. *Old Euston,* London, 1938

Taylor, S. *The Moving Metropolis. A History of London's Transport since 1800,* London, 2001
Thomas, R.H.G. *London's First Railway: The London & Greenwich,* London, 1972
Trench, R. & Hillman, E. *London under London. A Subterranean Guide,* London, 1985

Weightman, G. & Humphries, S. *The Making of Modern London, 1815-1914,* London, 1983
White, H.P. *A Regional History of the Railways of Great Britain. Vol 3: Greater London,* 3rd edition, Newton Abbot, 1987
White, J. *London in the Nineteenth Century,* London, 2007
Wolmar, C. *The Subterranean Railway. How the London Underground was built and how it changed the City forever,* London, 2004

Also available from Amberley Publishing

London Colour Archive

Brian Girling

ISBN 978-1-84868-222-1

£17.99

Full colour throughout,
250 colour postcards

Also available from Amberley Publishing

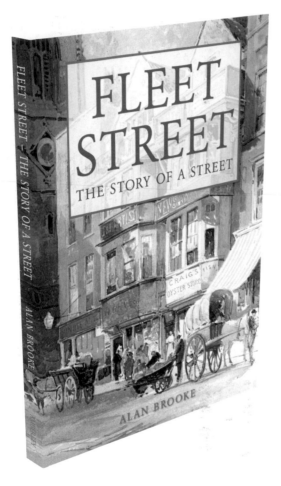

Fleet Street
The Story of a Street

Alan Brooke

ISBN 978-1-84868-229-0
£12.99

Available from all good bookshops or order direct
from our website www.amberleybooks.com

Also available from Amberley Publishing

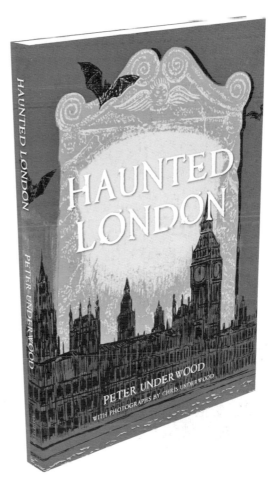

Haunted London

Peter Underwood

ISBN 978-1-84868-262-7

£12.99

Available from all good bookshops or order direct
from our website www.amberleybooks.com

Coming soon from Amberley Publishing

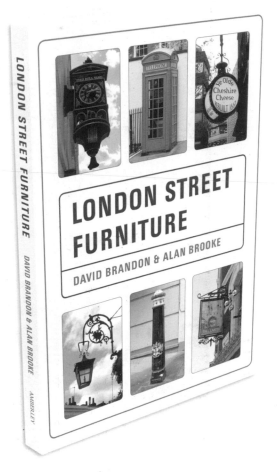

London Street Furniture

David Brandon &
Alan Brooke

ISBN 978-1-84868-294-8
Publication date: July 2010